THE FIRST TRI: AS A YOUNG MAN

THE FIRST TRI:
As a Young Man

DAN FISHWICK

PALMETTO
PUBLISHING
Charleston, SC
www.PalmettoPublishing.com

© 2024 Dan Fishwick

All rights reserved.

No portion of this book may be reproduced, stored in a retrieval system, or transmitted in any form by any means–electronic, mechanical, photocopy, recording, or other–except for brief quotations in printed reviews, without prior permission of the author.

Hardcover ISBN: 9798822968677
Paperback ISBN: 9798822960435

TABLE OF CONTENTS

Beginnings 1

School Days and Hard Knocks 23

Out of Africa 85

Going Together 103

Settling In 125

PROLOGUE

*I*f any collection of writing deserves or demands some preliminary form of explanation, here it is. When I opened a card from my children on my birthday, New Year's Eve, it took me back to my days, a long time ago, of teaching English in middle school. In this memory, however, I'm not sure whether I was the teacher or the eighth grader in the third row. You see, my gift was a book of maybe 450 pages… depending. I haven't seen it. The book came with a hook, you might say. I had to write the book, week by week, in response to the prompts that my loving children and their spouses provide. These are to be submitted to the publisher, week by week, for my family's reading pleasure. At the end of the year the publisher would print a copy (up to 450 pages) for each of them. So that's the premise, that's the gift, and you can imagine how this might have gone over with that eighth-grade student on the first day of school.

Well, I can imagine. My family I think sensed something from my response, something like horror, at what this entailed. They told me two other fathers or in-law fathers had agreed to this birthday gift and were well on their way to writing the great American memoir. That, too, was a little disappointing, the fact that they took up the task without a fight. Guess that's the eighth grader in me. As I looked around the living room that birthday night, at those eager faces, I knew it was too late to change schools, and they were just too damn eager for me to say no. But the assignment had to come with a couple caveats. Number one: no week-to-week submissions. You readers will have to wait. Number two: I do have a lot to say (brace yourselves), but what I choose to write may or may not be inspired by the well-considered prompts offered.

Any number of studies related to brain activity tell us that writing is among our most difficult mental tasks. In my teaching of writing, that conclusion was obvious. (You might be interested in knowing that at the bottom of brain activity is watching TV, just above sleeping.) When I write, I become consumed in the process. At the desk, in the field or at home, I think about what I'm working on, where it came from, how it sounds, whether I nailed it or buried the idea in vagaries, and where do we go from here. That's the source of my horror, knowing that as long as this takes me (a year?), my "book" will demand an enormous amount of mental focus and attention. I have been wanting to write a few things down before I run out of new years, and maybe that's why I didn't persist in my adolescent fight against hard work and agreed to take this on. But I do have some sense of the cost.

Dan Fishwick
Jan '24

CHAPTER 1

*M*y initial prompt is to write about my earliest memories. To me that raises the question of whether one needs language to form and sustain a memory. If so, that explains why so many of our earliest recollections don't seems to surface until we are at least three or older. And the ones we do recall from long ago would probably be highly sensory experiences if not traumatic. You know from observing your household dogs and cats that they have memory, even if they can't tell you the story. But there wouldn't be any details for them to cling to, and their memories will be a reaction to something they smell or hear, a friendly hand, a ride in the car, the nasty mailman who comes every day and makes a racket on the porch. Our own very early memories are not unlike those. That is until we start using words to tell. When we have words, we might add details, and if there were a photograph, that would clinch it, lock it forever in those layered recesses of gray matter.

The writer James Joyce is/was arguably the foremost master of the English language. His autobiography, *Portrait of the Artist as a Young Man,* begins with his earliest memory, and we can see how sensitive Joyce is to the need for language:

"Once upon a time and a very good time it was there was a moocow coming down along the road and this moocow that was coming down along the road met a nicens little boy named baby tuckoo... . His father told him that story: his father looked at him through a glass: he had a hairy face. He was a baby tuckoo. The moocow came down the road where Betty Byrne lived: she sold lemon platt.
O, the wild rose blossoms On the little green place.
He sang that song. That was his song.
O, the green wothe botheth.
When you wet the bed first it is warm then it gets cold. His mother put on the oilsheet. That had the queer smell."

Yes, there are a lot of words here, but they are informed by the stories of his dad. And the memory itself is rich in sensual detail: the moocow, the hairy face, wild rose blossoms, his song, the warm then wet bed, the queer smell.

When I was that age, whatever it is, a few events were somewhat branded into my long-term memory, though I would not attempt to encase those memories in language. I remember being on my father's shoulders in the middle of Second Street among a large crowd, all watching a fire at Marshall's Drugstore on the other side of Main. That's it. Nothing to add. I'm sure I could feel the heat, and the streets were probably a cacophony of firetrucks, crowd chatter, police orders, water-hoses and flame. If I were telling the story, I would embellish those sense experiences, but I'm not sure I remember any of that.

Our town of Willoughby in the early 1950s had a small airport a couple miles west of town. They hosted a yearly airshow featuring vintage double-winged planes, aerial acrobatics, and all manner of stunts while in the air. My older brothers were in scouts at the time, and I think my father may have been scoutmaster. Apparently I tagged along that day. We sat in the grass on a rise across the street. That's where the hospital is today and the airfield is now a mélange of fast foods, clinics, and strip malls on the other side of Euclid Avenue. The planes overhead roared and did loop-de-loops, much to the thrill of the onlookers who ooh-ed and ah-ed, as each part of the program became more an act of daring the devil. As we were watching, someone in the crowd noticed a lot of confetti coming from one of the planes. Soon we were all focused and saw that the confetti turned out to be shreds of the wing. And then the plane went down with a crash, somewhere in the fields below.

This is where my memory gets fuzzy because what happened next seems so out of time that I doubted what I saw, buried it for a long time, and much later as an adult had to ask my brother if what I remembered really happened. It did. After the crash, the boy scout troop, with me tagging along, went across the road, out into the overgrown fields to have a look at the wreckage. I saw things I shouldn't have seen, twisted rubble and body parts. I must have buried that memory, because it didn't make any sense that I could have been there, that any of us should have been out in that field that day. I did not have a long discussion with my brother when I asked him about it not long ago. It may have affected him the same way as a ten-year-old. He simply said, yep, it happened.

When I was maybe four and my younger brother Bob two, we went to my grandmother's house on East 93rd Street in Cleveland while my mother was in the hospital. It's where my mother grew up, and in the 30s the neighborhood was nearly all Irish, all good parishioners of St. Thomas Acquinas. But after the war, my mother and her siblings married and split to the suburbs, leaving my grandmother and her son Jack, a lovable uncle with Downs, back in the hood which was changing rapidly. Her house was three stories high, dark inside, with oak paneling and a stained-glass window at the landing going upstairs. At this point in her life, I don't think my grandmother had a clue what to do with two little boys. She lived a simple and pious life, long after she buried her husband and raised her six children on her own through the depression. It wasn't easy, I know. To me she was austere and somewhat distant, but probably in those days I viewed most adults in the same way.

For some reason I vividly remember several events or experiences from our relatively brief time there. In the kitchen one afternoon I asked her what she was cooking on the stove. She snapped at me and said it was not proper for little boys to ask such questions. Okay. But why did that memory stay with me? When my

THE FIRST TRI: AS A YOUNG MAN

Bob and Dan with the big catch, mid-fifties

grandmother did laundry, the two little boys had to go to the basement with her. It was big and clean, but dark and damp. At some point down there, nature was calling me, and Grandmother was not done with the clothes. When I asked, she pointed to a galvanized pail in the corner, and there I sat to do my business, though I'm sure I didn't linger. That kind of memory stays with you.

Every day at Grandmother's on East 93rd a tired looking Black man rode down the street in a horse-drawn wagon, shouting in sing-song voice, "Paper! Rags!" It didn't come out quite so clearly, and it took me a long time (I mean much later) to get what he shouted. But a horse-drawn wagon? That was pretty exciting.

The other event at grandmother's that stuck with me may have been toward the end of our stay. I can remember the back door of the place, and as we were going out one day, my little brother had the top of his middle finger smashed when grandmother closed the door on it. He needed treatment, there was blood, and poor grandmother was mortified. We were very happy to be heading home.

CHAPTER 2

Our family moved to Willoughby in 1947, just six months after I was born. During the war they had lived in Hamilton Ohio where I and my brothers were born. My mother spent a lot of time with her in-laws while my dad served in the Navy, and, from what she told me, it was not a happy time for her. If I were to speculate, I'd say she felt isolated. I doubt if my mother had ever before associated with someone who was not Catholic. Now she was swept off her feet by a Baptist from downstate, and then had to live with his family in his absence. She did make friends, yes, Catholic friends, but I don't think she ever warmed up to a settled relationship with my dad's family, and, sorry to say, I never got to know them very well myself.

Jordan Drive in Willoughby was a post-war, dead-end street of forty-eight little houses, twenty-four lining each side. I came to know a lot about the neighborhood because I delivered the local newspaper to all but four of those houses, starting at age seven. My two older brothers had had the route before me, but they took early retirement. Mr. Avery worked for the paper and came to the house every week to pick up the collections, minus the paperboy's take. He was a kindly older man and always seemed quite at home when he sat in our kitchen with a cup of coffee and change spread out over the kitchen table. When my next oldest brother, Steve, gave the route up, Mr. Avery suggested that I take it. In the present world of all-adult deliverers and dying newspapers, the idea of a seven-year-old folding, stacking, carrying and collecting for forty plus customers seems like a world away. But I had that job for the next six years and can probably tell stories about every one of those forty-eight houses and the residents. Don't worry, I won't.

Dick Mele and Rick Uritus are left and right; four Fishwicks in the middle.

We lived in the second house on the right, which was also at the top of the hill that sloped its way to the end of the street, toward the sign that said "Dead End", with a cornfield beyond. Jordan is just off of US-20, which we call Euclid Avenue. Euclid Avenue begins in downtown Cleveland and ends just a couple blocks from the top of our street. Route 20, however, is/was a coast-to-coast US highway, and, on lazy summer days, we would sit on the grassy corner near the mailbox and count out-of-state license plates of vacationers as they passed on the road.

That brings up a related story from those days. There was a local man named Willie who was, as we now say, developmentally delayed. My guess is that every town had their Willie who was just part of the fabric of town life. Willie always carried an impressive belt of mechanical tools around town and happily greeted anyone around. One day an out-of-state car broke down in front of Mrs. Cobb's house, a couple blocks away, stranding a family who was eager to be on their way. They must have felt relieved when they saw Willie with his friendly smile and his impressive leather tool belt. He offered his help, and they needed help. Willie got right to work. He unbolted, unscrewed, and pulled wires, of anything that could be unbolted, unscrewed or pulled, setting the various parts on the sidewalk as he went. After an hour or so, Willie stepped back, smiled, and said "Nope, can't figure out what's wrong." And he went happily on his way. I never heard what became of the family and their travels.

The houses on Euclid Avenue were not at all like our post-war bungalows on Jordan Drive. From Cleveland to Willoughby there stretched an incredible array of architectural gems dating from

Cleveland's industrial hey-day of the late nineteenth and early twentieth centuries. The largest homes and the most ostentatious were on "Millionaires Row" in Cleveland. At the time, this stretch of Euclid was considered to be the greatest concentration of wealth in the world. By the nineteen-fifties, ninety percent of these majestic places were gone, knocked down, burned up and bulldozed for "progress."

But twenty miles away down Euclid Avenue, two old Victorian homes stood like sentinels at the top of Jordan Drive. On the left was the Scanlon Tourist Home where my Hamilton grandparents stayed during a rare Thanksgiving visit which happened to coincide with an historic snowstorm. I still have an image, looking through a downstairs window, of two dark figures on a blanket of white, trudging through deep snow from the tourist home to our house at the top of Jordan. The Scanlon house has recently undergone a significant renovation/restoration, and is now divided into workplaces for small businesses who rely on social networking and advanced computer skills. No one seems to have heard of the name Scanlon.

On the opposite side of Jordan Drive, on Euclid Avenue, was the Hogan family. Mr. Hogan owned Hogan Packard, a car dealership. The families down the street, many of whom were escapees of pre-war city life, regarded the Hogans as aristocrats, like a local branch of the Kennedy family, long before JFK was on our radar. There were six Hogan children in this grand Victorian home. Out front were massive old beech and oak trees, and along the Jordan Drive side of Hogan's was a border of mature cedars. In the back were rows of grape vines next to a small pasture for their two horses. The large barn, with a lighted basketball court in front, was our favorite playground. One side of the barn was for cars, space for two, lined up end to end, perfect for indoor roller hockey. Adjacent to our hockey ring were the horse stalls.

On the other side of Euclid Avenue from the Hogan's was the Catholic church and school, Immaculate Conception, and the Hogan family was one of its pillars. But not unlike the Kennedys, the Hogan family suffered a number of tragedies. Dan Hogan of Hogan Packard died unexpectedly, leaving his wife and six children. I don't have any memory of him. A few years later, his oldest son, Dan Jr., a star quarterback for St. Joe's High School, developed leukemia and passed away in his senior year. I remember riding my bike (so I was old enough for that) with his brother Billy that day. We didn't know what else to do when we heard the news of Dan, so we rode around and around and around the circular drive of a Euclid Avenue neighbor. Years later, after hearing bad news, I similarly find myself out splitting wood with a mall, blow by blow.

I was only inside the Hogan home a couple of times after that. Still with a degree of old elegance, the house felt tomb-like, as Mrs. Hogan had descended into depression and alcohol. The business was sold. The horses gone. The grapevines overgrown. Eventually the Hogan place was sold to the Baptist church next door to it. The house still stands, but it looks like a skeleton of its former, in my eyes, grandeur.

Meanwhile, down Jordan Drive, life in the fifties was bustling. For the boys, fifteen of us probably, the street was ours. We could sled the hill, play ball in the street, where the sewer in front of Courtot's was always first base, or hike to the dead end, across the corn field and beyond. There were girls, too, and I can name a few of them, but I don't remember any joining us in our ball-playing and trekking about.

The boundaries were inching out as we added years. When we said "uptown," that meant the heart of Willoughby's municipal and shopping district. For us "downtown" was Cleveland. Uptown was only four blocks away, and we were free to make it part of our roaming, as long as we made it home for supper. We also jumped over the chain link fence behind Rick Uritus's house on the other side of Jordan to land on the Van Gorder estate—and a real estate it was. The house up front on Euclid Avenue was a massive sandstone construction designed by Charles Schweinfurth, a well-known Cleveland architect, around 1900. We never knew the very elderly Van Gorders, but we loved to explore the acres behind the house leading down to a small pond. That's where you'd find us on cold winter days, two boots at each end for goals, playing hockey all day when we could. Our explorations were always accompanied by nervous looks to see if the dreaded gardener was about. The word "gardener" to us got mixed up with garter snake. Both seemed like something we should avoid, more the gardener than the snake. I don't think the gardener ever bothered us in winter during hockey season, but I recall an incident in another season where the gardener performed his ritualistic duty of making us go away.

Generally, those chases were routine and harmless. But one day brother Bob and Rick and I were a bit surprised when the gardener seemed to appear out of the blue and close to us. We took off, and Rick and I had safely landed in Rick's back yard, when we realized that slower Bob had been nabbed, probably to the shock of both the gardener and Bob. There were all kinds of cellars, window wells and outbuildings on the estate, which we knew to be torture chambers. Our imaginations went wild as we sat in the back near the fence and mourned Bob's demise. Not long after, we heard Bob clambering over the fence, big smile on his face and a pocket full of candy. "He's a nice guy," he said. And he didn't show any evidence of the tortures he must have endured.

Rick Uritus, Dan and Bob

The other expansion of our territory was getting beyond the "dead-end" sign at the bottom of the street and out across the corn field to the storied place of hobo camps along the railroad tracks. We may have been twenty years too late to catch up with the mythical hoboes, but it was a daring thing to have a look. My older brother Steve, who was probably tired of trying to keep up with the eldest, Dave, thought it would be great if just he and I, four years younger, took the hike on our own. He made peanut butter and jelly sandwiches on Tip-Top Bread, and stuffed them into a WWII surplus knapsack. It was a very hot day, and we walked and walked. I think we made it to the tracks, but we had no idea where we were or what we were looking for. The sandwiches came out of the knapsack flattened like roadkill. That was too much for Steve and his dreams of charting new territory. He sat down and cried. That's all I remember, but the memory stayed with me over the years. I was never personally frightened about being lost, not when you're on a railroad track, but I was very moved by my brother's fragility in the face of dashed hopes and felt closer to him for it.

CHAPTER 3

What I remember most about our family life on Jordan Drive and later Park Avenue is now more of an assumption of how it must have been rather than an actual memory. In each of those houses were three bedrooms for the six of us. One bath. That was standard in those days, and many were happy to have that space. I always roomed with my younger brother Bob; Steve with Dave. One fact that I have to throw into this cozy equation is that in my middle school years, for instance, there were four smokers (parents and brothers) who were a few years short of the memo about taking it outside. Our place and everyone in it must have reeked. But that was standard in those days.

Mealtimes were something of a feeding frenzy. Each of my brothers grew to be six feet three, and though I didn't aspire to such heights, I ate my share. My mother was a fifties frozen food gal in the kitchen. Her vegetables came from the freezer, potatoes and cakes from a box, cheese from Velveeta. But depending on the day of the week, there was plenty to eat. Saturday, right after shopping, was the peak time, descending through the week to meatless Fridays and probably a tuna casserole made with Campbell's mushroom soup. The dinner table always had on it a plate of very white Wonder Bread next to a dish of margarine and a jar of grape jam. In a pinch you could always knock down a couple of those.

My mother was very thin. She liked it that way, but the downside is that Louise never acquired the love of preparing and eating good food. And here she was, charged with feeding five men. It was meat and potatoes all the way, maybe a package of Birdseye and some iceberg. We all ate together, whoever was home, but we didn't linger around the table past the first cigarette.

One aspect of our family that might not have been "standard in those days" was the amount of fighting that was tolerated. My parents fought, my brothers fought, I fought them. The noise level and the drama of these scenes was downhome epic. With one exception, I don't recall any attenuating violence resulting from this rather steady din nor any lasting effects on our fraternal friendships. The exception was toward the end of my father's drinking days, and we'll give that a rest. But I have come to believe that all the noisy rancor was unnecessary, even though I don't understand its underlying causes.

Or maybe I'm being too sensitive or selective in what I remember. The photos tell a very different story, especially the ones taken on our family vacations. August family camping trips were something of a tradition. We packed up whatever wagon we had at the time with tents, sleeping bags, cooking gear, Coleman stoves and lanterns, and the six of us would head to the Adirondacks, or up to North Bay in Ontario, or to Hartwick Pines in northern Michigan. Pulling this off successfully with four boys of different ages requires planning and efficient execution. My parents did this and enjoyed it. And the four of us, as our different poses show, with stringers of fish or next to the falls, were very much enjoying each other and the places we went.

Not everyone is aware that there are Catholic shrines along the route defined above. For instance, you can get to Isaac Jogues in upstate New York or go all the way to Ste. Anne de Beaupre in Quebec. And there's a replica of Lourdes up in Michigan. This was my mother's payback—we visited each one and others with pictures to prove it.

A shrine from the fifties, somewhere in America

A key to finding self and sanity in crowded if not uncomfortable situations is to find and carve out a niche, a good place to observe from, not attractive enough to bring in company, far enough removed to be able to immerse oneself in other pursuits. For me, that was my big oak desk next to the furnace in the basement on Park Avenue. Our basement was divided. On one side was a finished rec-room with tile floor and built-in bookshelves featuring a shrine of Mary. On the other side of the knotty pine walls was the worktable and vise, a few tools, the furnace and my desk. Here I did my homework and built and tuned in to a Heathkit short wave radio, made models, read Popular Mechanics. On warm days in the summer, I slept in the basement, too, on the other side, under the Virgin's watchful eye.

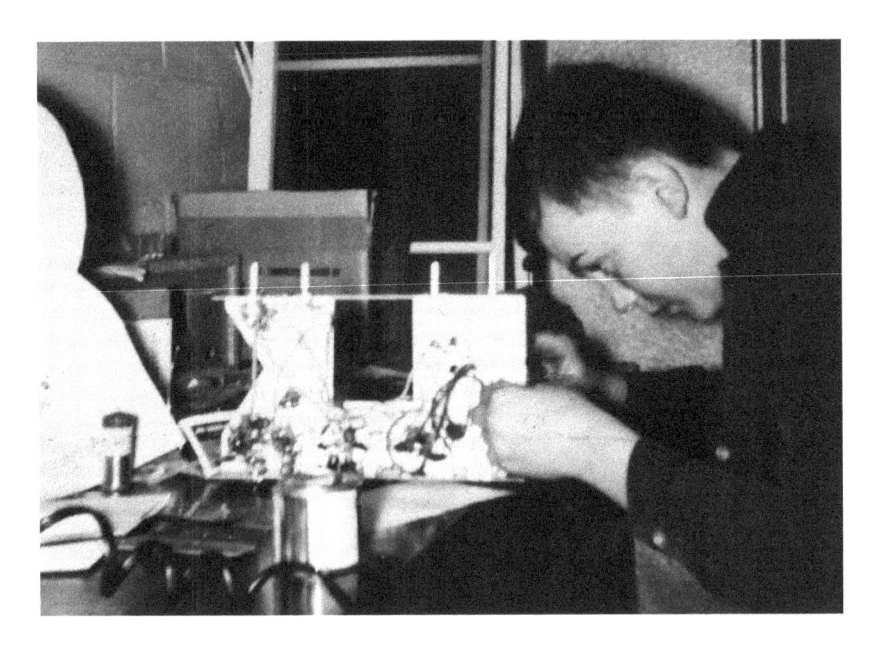

At work near the furnace, circa seventh grade

Another natural hiding place for my reticent ways was simply my place in the lineup. My oldest brother, Dave, was hard at work being the oldest, trying his best to wear the mantel of responsibility. Steve made a good effort to keep up with Dave, but he cloaked his ultimate resignation with humor and became the class clown in school. Their academic struggles generally required a good deal of my parents' attention. So when I came along after a hiatus of four years since Steve was born, I received the blessing of benign neglect. I didn't have to be the oldest or a struggling second, and Bob would follow me to become the "baby of the family" and get whatever attention was left over. My parents were busy and I was free to cruise.

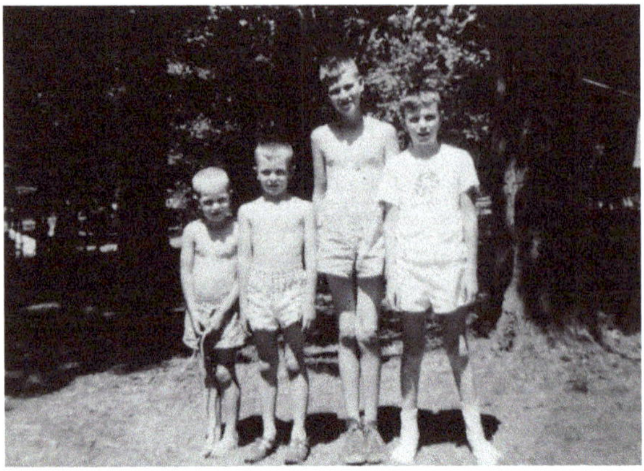

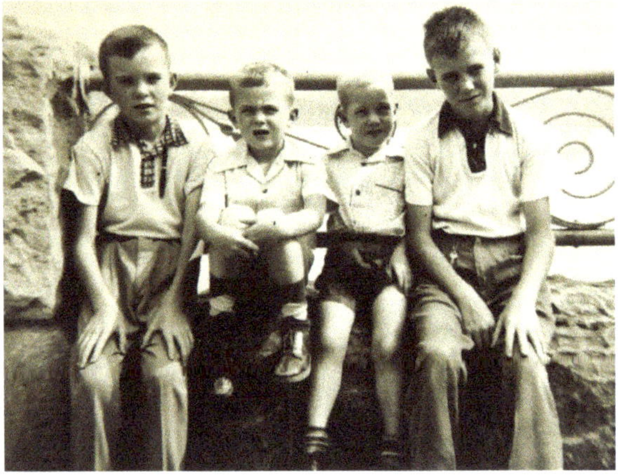

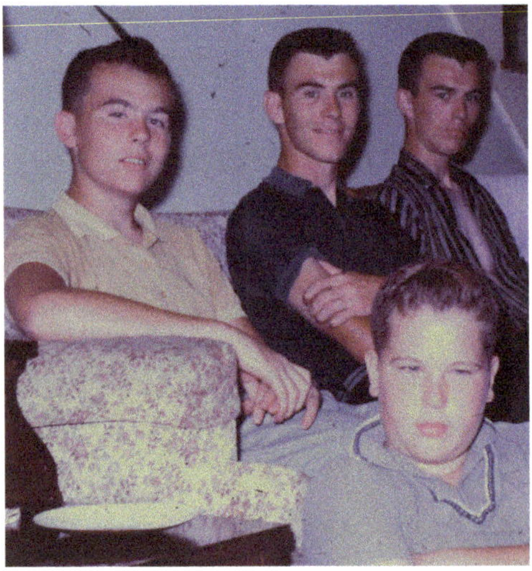

School Days and Hard Knocks

CHAPTER 4

*I*mmaculate Conception School had no kindergarten, so we all enjoyed an extra year of backyard freedom; and, personally, I'd like to think my education was enhanced by that gift of time. But starting school gets us well beyond the "Dead End," and the world expands exponentially. The parish school, ICS as we called it, was less than two hundred yards from our front door, so I never rode a school bus until I drove one as a teacher many years later. In fact, those of us who lived close to the school went home for lunch, where we could wolf down what our stay-at-home mothers fixed for us, catch a little of Captain Penny and the "little rascals" on TV, and still make it back to the schoolyard in time to get in a few games. My first-grade class, along with all the other first grade classes across the country, was at the forefront of the baby boom. School buildings would begin to bulge and whole neighborhoods would appear out of overgrown fields. Staid old Willoughby and ICS in particular saw the arrival of Italians, Poles, Irish, Hungarians, and, like my family and maybe the majority, a healthy post-war mongrel mix.

It surprises me to hear someone say they don't recall any of their grade school teachers. My memory has never been stellar, but I remember every one of them. Perhaps that's because we spent every day, all day (except for lunch) in a classroom with one adult. There were no specials then, no tutors, no counselors, no art or phys-ed teachers. The only administrator I recall was the principal, the convent mother, who also taught. So that gave us a lot of time to study the one adult in large classes of thirty or forty children. Of the eight teachers in those eight years, two were forgettable even if I can't; two were lovable and important and timely in what they taught me about reading, math and kindness. The remaining four left an indelible mark.

Sister Lucia was my first-grade teacher. She must have been very young, although that's hard for a six-year-old to determine, especially considering the habits of Ursuline nuns in the fifties. Their robes were all black, long and flowing, but they had a stiff, white covering of their foreheads and a starched bib below their chins. What I could see of Sister Lucia was rosy youth. Most kids in those days came to first grade without knowing how to read, and probably had not played with alphabet blocks. That would be me, and Sister Lucia took me on my way. But what I remember most about Sister Lucia was what she could do with a piece of chalk and a blackboard. When we read Dick and Jane, she would stand by the board and draw out the figures from the story, and they looked better than the ones in the book. I couldn't believe my eyes and thought that was a talent all nuns had, or all teachers, or any adults besides my parents. I came to find out later that Sister Lucia had gone on to publish coloring books and then became a beloved art teacher at Beaumont High School into her nineties.

THE FIRST TRI: AS A YOUNG MAN

The "flutophone" was the first musical instrument I played, and that was in the first grade. It was a plastic recorder that was soft in the mouth and had a somewhat bitter taste. Well, at least it left a bitter taste. I began my accordion lessons in the second grade. We borrowed a small, black twelve-bass instrument from Arrowhead Music on Clark Street behind the main drag of town and signed up with a Mr. Sylvester to teach me. The accordion came with a boxy case, and it was clear to me that I wasn't strong enough to carry the instrument to town for my lesson. It was never a question of our parents dropping us off in a car—Dad was at work, Mom didn't drive. But I found my younger brother's worn and outgrown stroller in the corner of the garage. The canvas seating was somewhat shredded, so I tore the rest of it out, put the boxed accordion in, and strolled to my lesson in town. Mr. Sylvester got quite a kick out of this seven-year-old and let me know that he would always have another accordion at the studio for lessons, and I didn't have to bring mine every time.

By the third grade the baby boom bulge was getting serious. The powers that be were calling for reinforcements, and they hired Miss Clark, eighty-three years old, a retired teacher from Cleveland who took the Greyhound bus every day to Willoughby. She did not have enough command of her own faculties to be in the least sense convivial. Her desk in the classroom was elevated, and from that perch, with seating chart in hand, she would call us by name and conduct class. If you happened to sit in Mary's seat instead of your own, you were Mary for the day. I suspect her eyesight wasn't so good either.

For most of Miss Clark's career as a third-grade teacher, she specialized in the next step beyond the printed word of the first grade and cursive in the second. That step was the fountain pen. Does anyone even know what I'm talking about? It was a big deal then. By this time our society had moved beyond ink wells and plumes. In fact, some Esterbrook and Schaeffer pens came with replaceable cartridges, which meant you did not have to pump up the ink to the pen's internal bladder. Do you really have any idea? But here's the thing. Sometime during the third grade, ball point pens came on the scene. Glorious. However, they were quickly banned in Miss Clark's third grade classroom, even though I don't think I ever used a fountain pen to do homework after that. Remember, Miss Clark didn't see so well. Miss Clark taught for yet another year, though I don't know how she came to deal with the loss of this key component of her curriculum.

One other note about Miss Clark. The bus-stop across from the school on Euclid Avenue, happened to be very near where my newspapers were deposited for me to deliver. I'd see Miss Clark sometimes at the stop in the afternoon, of course after spending the day with her. I'd greet her, say "Hello, Miss Clark," and it was clear, even to this nine-year-old, that she had no idea who I was.

Most of my career was spent teaching seventh and eighth grade, and maybe it was due to my own indelible experiences in those years that convinced me of the huge significance of that age. The religions and indigenous cultures of the world have long recognized this. Christians are confirmed, Jews are bar mitzvah-ed, young warriors are included in the hunt. Somehow our modern society has elevated the driver's license at sixteen or voting or drinking later to mean something similar. There's no comparison.

Charlie Moore was my seventh-grade teacher. He was rather slightly built, with oversized horn-rimmed glasses. Charlie lived with his parents and was probably a closeted or celibate homosexual. I didn't know the meaning of that then, though "homo" was a word bandied about by my more physically developed seventh grade classmates. Putting thirty-five to forty boys (boys and girls were separated in 7th and 8th grades at ICS) into a classroom with Charlie sounds like a recipe for disaster. It wasn't. In the classroom, Charlie was clear-eyed and in command. He had a powerful voice, a magnificent tenor, and when he sang "Oh Holy Night" at midnight Mass on Christmas every year, he looked ten feet tall and brought tears to the congregation.

The most memorable part of his curriculum was our afternoons every day. Charlie was a great lover of grand opera, and after we returned from lunch, this rag-tag group of miscreants would be handed a libretto and Mr. Moore would play LPs (That's a 33RPM record album, lately called vinyl.). We would listen while reading the stories of Puccini, Verdi, Rossini and others, going through each opera that the New York Metropolitan would bring to Cleveland in the spring. Charlie gave us our first introduction to foreign language, an acceptable version of sex education, a new approach to literature, and a bit about European history, to say nothing of the music that conveyed it. When the productions arrived in April, Charlie would load up his old Mercury with six or seven boys and take a different group each night down to Public Auditorium in Cleveland to experience grand opera of the Metropolitan company. I don't know what stayed with the other kids from this experience, after all, it was a rag-tag bunch. And I know Charlie couldn't get away with that use of time in these days of performance-measuring and proficiency exams. But to me, Charlie Moore gave a gift of culture that opened a much wider window to the world beyond. A college degree must not have been a requirement to teach in a parochial school at the time. Charlie kept at it, going to college nights and summers, but I know I graduated from college a few years before he did. He was a remarkable teacher.

The boys apparently outnumbered the girls in the eighth grade going into 1960, and a scheme was created to balance the act. Eight of the more tame and docile boys (or so it appeared to the rest of us) moved over to the girls' classroom which I think had the principal, Sister Thomasina, as their teacher. The boys went to Harry Johnson, a young father of three with an engineering degree, who must have been desperate to make ends meet and took the job of teaching a self-contained class of forty boys. It was never a happy time for any of us, and never clear who had control in that close and now stifling classroom. I was as lost as most kids that age, but this eighth-grade situation was beyond that and not easy to negotiate. Here I was trying to keep cool with my classmates who were obviously moving toward adolescence more quickly than I, while at the same time trying to be the star student and exemplar of good behavior. That tightrope was thin and ultimately impossible to keep under my feet. The only answer was the passage of time…and escape. Over the years I have sat in the classrooms of similarly struggling teachers and found it hard to pinpoint exactly what makes some adults so irritating to young adolescents. But putting a large number of early teen boys into one room within four walls all day for a year is insane to begin with and surely leads to insanity.

To catalogue the reasons for the chaos in Harry Johnson's classroom would demand much more energy and a better memory than I have. However, my own view, whatever it was, changed one day toward the end of that year. On a rainy April school night I went with my dad to a new bakery in town, a business that my father was somehow connected with. We went to get bread. And there, at eight or nine at night, covered in flour and wearing a baker's hat, was my teacher, Harry Johnson. I came to understand that after teaching this band of rascals all day within the confines of those four walls, Mr. Johnson went to work making bread. Nothing wrong with that work, but the man must have been exhausted by it all. That night I mumbled a greeting but kept my head down and knew this changed everything. In spite of his struggles at school, some self-inflicted, this was a very good man. He left teaching after the year and began his career in an electronics manufacturing firm. A good move for that good man.

Immaculate Conception School shut down some years ago. The rectory where the three priests, a pastor and two assistants, resided was leveled and is now a green lawn which is at times populated by little white crosses commemorating the lost souls of aborted babies. A sidewalk down the middle still leads up to, well, nothing. The convent on the other side of the church campus, where twelve to fourteen Ursuline nuns had lived, is currently the residence of a single priest. The good sisters aged and passed away without replenishment in their numbers. Mass is still said in the large church that my parents helped build in 1959, but the school of six hundred or so students is quiet and stands empty. Eight years I spent in that one building. Sounds like a lot of time, that is until a bit later when I taught in another building for thirty years.

Building the new church in Willoughby, 1959

CHAPTER 5

Before I move out and on to high school, I probably need to back up and talk about the family of four boys, second house on the right. Going way back, my father grew up in Hamilton, down near Cincinnati between an older brother, Tom, and a younger sister "Weezie," so-called because my father, young Paul, couldn't pronounce "Geneva." Fishwick is an old English name. There seem to be a number of them still in Lancastershire, and even a couple towns in northern England bear the name. Personally, I have never met a Fishwick that I am not related to, though I did correspond once with an Episcopal priest from Virginia with that name. In high school Paul chose a somewhat unusual path of courses—secretarial skills—which probably put him in class with mostly young women. Clever guy. Out of school he was employed in the insurance industry where he worked in one capacity or another for the rest of his life. He met my mother on an insurance-related trip to Cleveland, and they married in 1940.

Evelyn Louise Hurley, my mother, was born in Cleveland behind her twin sisters. The twins always struck me as serious and focused. I think they took their education and life generally more seriously than my mother who considered the depression a good time, even though her father (Daniel James, my namesake) had died in 1930 and her mother struggled to achieve some degree of equilibrium. Louise who, like her siblings, was called by her middle name, loved to dance and sing, and her stories from the time were usually celebrations of social gaiety. So when this rather suave and handsome-in-a-Bogart-sense guy from down-state strolled into the office where she worked in Cleveland, one can see how she might have been smitten.

Trying to imagine one's parents as young and in love is more difficult once we know the whole story that didn't end happily ever after. Well enough, I suppose. But their youth is a long way away, I wasn't there and have to trust the lovely old photos from their courting days.

Romance in a canoe July - 1940

Paul and Louise, acourtin', early 1940s

As I mentioned, Paul was also a Baptist, and in those days there could be no church ceremony for them. Officiated by a priest, of course, the vows were exchanged in the afternoon (also required) on the steps of the rectory, not in the sanctuary. I don't have any memory of whatever friction they may have felt in the first ten years of what was called a mixed-marriage. But around 1950 my father converted to Catholicism. And this wasn't at all like dragging him in: he embraced the faith, swallowed it whole. Within the parish he took on the mantle of the Holy Name Society and the Knights of Columbus. He led the family, Mom and four boys, in novenas of rosaries on the kitchen floor (damn hard on the knees) and installed living-room and basement shrines.

But Paul had his demons, too. He took the Greyhound or later a company car to downtown Cleveland every day to his insurance work. In the early fifties, though I was only vaguely aware, Paul was coming home later and later, after he had had way too much to drink on the way. I don't know what caused him to get on the wagon, but like his other conversion, it was whole. He left his job in Cleveland, joined AA and spent the rest of his life going to meetings and helping others cope with the disease. The example that Paul set for us boys impacted us for the rest of our lives.

At about this time, late-fifties, the family moved one block east of Jordan Drive to Park Avenue where our house was, yes, still second on the right. The house, a newer ranch, seemed much bigger than the old one, but in square footage, I'm not so sure. It was certainly more conducive to entertaining, and my parents loved to entertain. The church grounds stretched between Park and Jordan on the other side of Euclid, so we were still within sight of Immaculate Conception. And because of my parents' burgeoning associations with the life of the church, one parish priest or visiting missionary after another came to our house for dinner. In fact, we had one set of china reserved for such occasions, the "priest dishes."

I'm setting the stage here, you see. In the midst of all the chaos of my eighth-grade experience with Harry Johnson and my peers, I was applying to go into the seminary to become a parish priest. The reasons seem obvious now. When you've assisted a priest as an altar boy at 6:30 mass in the morning, played golf with the priest and your dad in the afternoon, and have had dinner with said priest at home in the evening under the painting of the Sacred

Heart of Jesus, you get bent in a certain direction. Our school, ICS, only went to the eighth grade. So all us were in a position to have to make a choice. Most of the kids probably went to public school. A number of them, as my brothers before me, went to St. Joe's High School on the eastern edge of Cleveland, a hike but doable. No one else from Willoughby chose to go to the minor seminary as I did that year, but there were others older than I from ICS already at Borromeo Seminary. Probably my hesitation in all this was my desire to play high school sports which took up a huge role in my life…and in my imagination. I think my father, in spite of his deep devotion to the church, harbored similar hopes for my athletic career, but he would never allow himself to get in the way of that decision. Sometime in late spring I received a letter of acceptance from Monsignor Whalen which also kindly suggested I avoid "mixed" company in the coming months before school. Not really a big problem for the likes of me.

The tradition at our grade school and many others was the trip to Geauga Lake on the last day of school. How that day would go was entirely predictable and a promise of fun. Why then did three of us decide to bicycle to Pennsylvania instead? John Franz and Bill Kloos, two friends from my class, joined me in the planning. I didn't pay attention to their negotiations for parental permission, but I knew it would be best for me to go to my father first and let him tell my mother. It worked, and we started to pore over roadmaps that would take us on back roads to Mercer, PA where I had second cousins of my mother's whom I had never met. Our bikes were typical kid bikes of the time, heavy, with fat tires, one speed and reverse brakes. We didn't know too much about much. We packed up a pound of baloney and a loaf of Wonder Bread, filled a couple army surplus canteens and left in the first light of morning. To say it was a long day would be a gross understatement. We chugged on and on, all day and into the dark. At about nine at night we came into Greenville, exhausted but with about ten miles to go and not enough light to see. There was a pay phone in front of the filling station where we stopped, and I called the Browns, my cousins. They were in the middle of a large graduation party on their farm on the Mercer-Greenville Road. But they said they'd send someone in a pick-up right away, and, "in the meantime, introduce yourself to John, your cousin who owns the gas station where you're calling from." It appears that I was related in one way or another to most of the people in Mercer County, where my grandparents had grown up.

We got to the Brown household as the party was winding down and folks were cleaning up. While we set up our pathetic pup-tent in the backyard, my aunt was cooking up eggs and pork chops, toast and jam for us, ravenous and nearly raving mad. The next morning, in much better spirits, we watched my uncle do his work in the shed out back. He was butchering a hog, and we saw the process from beginning to end before my parents arrived to visit and then take us home. It was the beginning of my own long relationship with the Browns and Hurleys of Pennsylvania. I never quizzed my other classmates about what they remember about their eighth-grade trip to Geauga Lake amusement park, but that day was for us unforgettable.

THE FIRST TRI: AS A YOUNG MAN

About to enter Borromeo Seminary, eighth grade grad

CHAPTER 6

*B*orromeo Seminary was only five or six miles from home, but it could have been on the other side of the world and a century away. As we have experienced before, our freshman class was the largest they had ever seen, numbering over a hundred. Some of those boys bailed in the first week; others have been priests now for over fifty years and are just retiring. They came from all over the diocese which includes Cleveland and Akron and all the surrounding suburbs in the metropolitan area.

Our dorms were generally two floors of long rows of beds adjacent to each other, eight beds on each side. Lockers, small but big enough for all we carried, stood in a cluster at the end of the room. Our two dorm priests, Fr. Liberatore and Fr. Murphy, lived in two tiny apartments on the first floor which also housed a large study hall where each of us had a desk, not an office desk mind, but a classroom desk with a little bookcase next to it. Hoban Hall was one corner of a quadrangle the size of a football field, but come to think of it, I never saw anyone play anything in that space. On our side of this quadrangle was the gym which faced the chapel and two other dorms on the other side. At either end of the rectangle was the classroom building and, opposite, the refectory, where we ate all our meals. There were large playing fields surrounding these buildings and a path up a hill behind the campus, with Stations of the Cross on the way. From a clearing at the top we could see in the distance ships passing on Lake Erie. Here we were standing on the foundation of what had been one of those grand Euclid Avenue mansions, atop the hill, with only odd sandstone steps going nowhere and bits of crumbling concrete scattered about.

For the first and only time in my life I experienced homesickness in those first weeks. I wasn't the only one, and some found it so unbearable they went home. It was a gnawing pain, exacerbated by the Friday night sounds of the local high school football game nearby. That's what I remember, listening in bed next to an open window for announcers, cheers, the band and feeling terrible, trying to grasp what was familiar outside while lying in one room among fifteen strangers. That gnawing pain was short-lived, however, and within weeks homesickness was a memory, like that of a childhood bout of flu, and we became accustomed to a life which was very different from our peers outside of the seminary.

For the next four years there was no television, radio or newspapers. We went home for Thanksgiving, Christmas and Easter, but otherwise centered our lives around that quadrangle. Once a week we could take a walk into town, if Wickliffe could be so-called. But as time went on, most of us weren't even inclined to do that—sports and studies were always pulling us in other directions.

Borromeo was a "minor" seminary. That is high school and all of the preparation that leads to taking vows and entering "major" seminary, a four-year post-college study of theology which concludes in ordination to the priesthood. Those later theology courses would require command of Latin, and some Greek and Hebrew, the languages of the ancient texts that were studied. So even at our level, how you fared in Latin often determined whether you moved on or were asked to leave. If you started the seminary after high school, you were required to spend your first year studying Latin to catch up.

Borromeo was a close environment. The teachers were all priests with the exception of Mr. Tighe, who taught phys-ed, health and coached basketball. Invariably the word "father" came out in addressing him since all our other teachers were "father." But he was a father of three and happily pointed that out each time. The priests were mostly in their twenties or thirties and had distinguished themselves academically, I suppose, because they did not move on to parishes like those who had been ordained with them. Many of the faculty were on a track that would lead to positions of higher responsibility within the diocese after their teaching days. They would become monsignors (before that title disappeared), bishops, scholars in theology, diocesan administrators. Teachers and students at the seminary, adults and kids generally, did not mingle and mix, as they seem to today. After all, in the fifties and sixties, there were a lot more of us than them. But our teacher/priests lived in the dorms with us and ate with us in the refectory; they walked the quadrangle in groups after dinner, just like we did in our own groups. Distant, but very close.

THE FIRST TRI: AS A YOUNG MAN

I spent two years in Hoban Hall, both as a freshman and later as a senior prefect, so I got to know Father Liberatore and Father Murphy very well. They were cut from a different cloth, so to speak. Father Liberatore's apartment had very nice carpeting, a stereo system divided into components (new to me), a rich leather chair for reading and art on the walls. He was young, suave and never averse to a good cigar. Father Murphy, at the other end of the hall, was his opposite. He was very tall and gaunt, a serious intellectual, who lived in a room so sparse it could only be compared to a cell, as in jail cell or monastery cell. I recall that Father Murphy once spent a much-needed vacation in Hawaii. He very soon found the Honolulu library and spent his fun time studying the Hawaiian language. After minor seminaries became a thing of the past in the late seventies, Father Liberatore became a parish pastor; Father Murphy the superintendent of schools in the diocese.

If there were twelve or fourteen priests comprising the faculty, I had every one of them as a teacher, most of them twice. Father Pilla, later Bishop Pilla, taught me in five courses in four years. I don't think any new teachers arrived or any old ones left in my four years, so with that intensity of close contact, you could say my teachers left a serious impression.

Our days began with a bell at 6:30 a.m., mass was at seven, but no one spoke before the blessing was said for breakfast. This was a part of the "Grand Silence." From the closing of evening prayers around 9:00 p.m. until breakfast the next day, we adhered to silence. And we did, mostly. We went to classes after breakfast and through the day until four, usually sitting in one classroom while the teachers rotated. Outside of the physics and biology labs, I can't remember any classroom identified with a particular teacher. We had classes six days a week including Saturdays, but Tuesdays and Thursdays we had off in the afternoon, time for a lot of sports, much study and the occasional walk down Euclid Avenue in Wickliffe. Dinner was followed by a two-hour study period before closing prayers in chapel. Most of us carried a paperback in our blazer pocket for the many times in the day we were required to move quietly. For the first half of lunch or evening dinner, a designated student reader would read from an elevated pulpit. I don't know which priest chose the books, but they were generally historical fiction and kept our attention while we clinked, clanked and chewed our way through the meal.

Toward the middle of our four years at Borromeo, the Catholic Church underwent a sea-change when Pope John XXIII called for a rare council of the church, Vatican II. As a result, mass was now to be said in the language of the people hearing it, not Latin. Gregorian chant, which I had studied for two years, was replaced by more singable folksy responses. Some centuries-old rituals were modernized, for lack of a better word, to become more meaningful to the people. John XXIII was very popular and he was canonized a saint in 2000. However, this move away from the old ways still rankles modern Catholic conservatives. Our teachers were probably more sensitive to these changes than we seminarians, but I think it may have produced a degree of restlessness in us as news of world events—civil rights and the Vietnam War— began to seep in to our cloistered lives.

Looking back, it may look like more of an explosion than a seeping in. Not so when you think about the explosion of adolescence itself from within each of us at the time, ages fourteen to eighteen. Decisions were being made in Washington by people named Dulles and McNamara and all believers in the domino theory that would affect America for generations, and still do. And in Rome, leaders of the Catholic faith were making decisions that would affect the world church for generations, and still do. But in my seminary days of the early sixties, we had yet to feel those effects. I think that would be true of most of America. We had inherited a nineteen-fifty's worldview, pretty comfortable for us in the postwar suburbs. Some of us heard Dylan at the time sing "the times, they are a changin." Some of us didn't.

I mentioned that I had Father Pilla for five courses in four years. When I was a junior and senior, he offered an elective course in Russian history. We carefully read Marx's Communist Manifesto and a number of, in my memory, very challenging tomes about Russian history. It's complex. But the underlying theme of the course, much highlighted and discussed, was Marx's and Lenin's pronounced atheism, the castigation of religion as the "opiate of the people." That rejection of religion became synonymous with communism worldwide. The U.S. mission in southeast Asia was part holy crusade, I believe, and at Borromeo, I was readying myself to join the warriors for religion, preparing the message. But if a point is to be made, it's that we are all products of and in most ways bound to the world we have come from and live in. The old world I knew and the seminary I lived in held me firmly. But the times, they were changing.

Today I enjoy several close friendships with men I met as boys in the ninth or tenth grade. It's easy to start up a conversation with someone you've lived with for four years, no matter what course our lives have taken since. Each of them carry their own memories, but when we gather it's surprising what we are able to reconstruct from that time long ago. For some of them I was equated with athletic achievement, though those are not so much memories I retain about myself. Yes, we had lots of sports at Borromeo and those did consume a fair amount of my time, but here there were no Friday night lights, no rallies and cheerleaders, just play on the field—flag football, basketball, track and softball, handball, ping-pong and pool. We did have an interscholastic basketball team and a good one, but it was tough to find real competition, since none of the schools wanted to risk injury in a non-league game, and they certainly did not want to risk losing to a team of seminarians. One athletic event that did stay with me was winning the school pentathlon as a senior. It consisted of high jump and long jump (my strengths), 100 yard dash (got a good jump at the line on that one), the mile and the shot put. Not much to show for the last two. My name was inscribed on a brass plate which hung somewhere for some time and now exists only in memory.

My earliest recollection of life at Borromeo was my role in the traditional ninth grade Latin play. We put on "Little Drummer Boy," and I was the little drummer. Featured was the eponymous song that began, "Come, they told me…," and I sang it in Latin, "Veni dicere, par umpa pum pum." I was worried about getting the words right, so I wrote them all out and taped them to the top of the snare drum. The bishop would be there in the first row,

THE FIRST TRI: AS A YOUNG MAN

checking out this batch of new seminarians. When the lights went down and I stepped to the front of the stage, I couldn't see a thing except the bishop in the first row and a sea of faces in the audience. I got through the opening, "Veni dicere…," but have no clue what followed. I think I ran through noun declensions and verb conjugations, the meanings of which escaped us all. Something like "Dare terra, par umpa pum pum, Amo terrae, par umpa pum pum." No one ever said a word about my performance.

After freshman year we could choose between two different courses of study. The path I chose was heavier in math and science courses—logic and trig, chemistry and physics. The other track was language centered, primarily the addition of French and Greek. I'm guessing we were evenly divided. Father Murphy (remember him?) taught both trigonometry as well as French, so there was no escaping his gaze in the classroom, a gaze down from his six-five frame. We all felt more than a little scrutinized in his presence; and in his logic/trig course, simply humbled.

One of the more outstanding characteristics of the school, in spite of operating in the vast shadow of the church hierarchy, was how many of our activities were student-controlled. There was no music program, per se, taught by adults, but our choral program was stellar. For the first two years we sang under the baton of a junior/senior student. He was demanding and brought out the best in us. He was replaced by a gifted classmate of mine who also could accompany us on piano. And along the way, I joined millions of others across the land and picked up a guitar, so I could play along with our newly formed quartet of folk singers. The intramural sporting program was also organized by students who formed the teams, listed the standings, played the games and served as refs. And I should add that most of the cleaning chores around school fell upon us, the students. The official maintenance staff was small and more concerned with heating and electrical infrastructure. Students played no role in the kitchen with food preparation, however. That was the vocation of a small group of nuns.

In spite of our semi-cloistered existence, it was never easy to find solitude at Borromeo. Even in silence we were surrounded. We had no rooms to ourselves. We slept in long rows of beds. Maybe that explains why a particular school project stands out in my memory. The biology classroom had the skeletons of several small animals, a snake, I think, skulls of rodents, probably even a human skeleton. I was intrigued and inspired. After the required dissection of a very large bull-frog, I boiled and bleached the bones and carefully reassembled and glued the joints. I put the frog into the position of leaping, so that the hind legs were stretched out, as if about to jump into an imagined pond. I enjoyed that work, using my hands to build things, something I missed from my pre-Borromeo days. But the best part of that project was being in an empty room by myself, on warm spring afternoons, totally absorbed in what I was doing, a rare treat.

In my junior year my brother Bob came in as a freshman. By this time my oldest brother Dave was married, and next oldest, Steve, had joined the army, so my parents were suddenly empty-nesters, and they worked together, too, in my father's independent insurance agency in Willoughby. No more commutes to Cleveland.

The result was they became much more involved in the civic affairs of Willoughby. Add Chamber of Commerce, Kiwanis, and Rotary Club to the list of my father's Catholic commitments. He was also a business partner of the mayor, so it wasn't hard for me to get a summer job with the city between my junior and senior years. I worked in the concession stand at Daniels Park, with an aspiring flautist (the mayor's daughter) on her way to college and a wacky college sophomore (son of a prominent local businessman) who was one of the funniest guys I've ever known. The flautist is to this day still teaching flute. Jimmy died in an auto accident that very fall.

Daniels Park, along the Chagrin River, was the local swimming hole behind the dam that crossed the river there. The lifeguard sat high up on a large concrete stand overlooking the dam along which, stretched across it from pole to pole, was a single guy-wire about waist high. This was meant to keep you from slipping off the dam into the eddies eight feet below. Closer to the pop stand, as we called it, were two concrete kiddie pools for those who weren't ready to tackle the muddy waters of the river. They were watched over by junior-lifeguards, among whom was a girl named Carol (daughter of the president of the board of education). Carol had blond hair and long legs which I had plenty of time to observe. When no one was in the pool she would drift over to the stand and we would talk, mostly about nothing, I'm sure, or play a game of chess over the counter. I was as much a curiosity to her as she was to me. She discovered in time that there were T-bone steaks buried beneath the ice-cream in the pop stand's freezer. I cooked one for her in the toaster-oven. She melted in delight. Carol lived on River Street, just above the hill overlooking Daniels Park, and that was on my way home. I walked her home a few times. Nothing happened really. I wouldn't have known what to do. Come August and September, she was back at South High, the local public school, and I went back to Borromeo.

For me there was no wavering in my commitment to become a Catholic priest. I was as dedicated a student as ever, but things really were changing, outside and in. Our class of a hundred had dwindled to forty-eight in our senior year. After graduation the numbers would be halved again. That meant that half the senior class was at loose ends trying to figure out where they were going after leaving the seminary. And the seminary didn't seem to have a plan to deal with this contingent. You see, it was assumed you stayed in the seminary until you decided not to and simply left. That day. Not so practical if you were in your last year of high school at a place you had come to love. College counseling was not a part of the seminary program.

These impending changes for each of us had the effect of our stretching some of the rules, questioning old folkways, and involving everyone in our excitement that we were indeed moving on, all of us. Outside the walls, the issues of civil rights and Vietnam were demanding our participation, and family meals across the land were becoming generational debates. On a minor note, I remember the Thanksgiving break in the fall of that year, 1964. My eighth grade bicycling friend, John Franz, now had his driver's license and we loved to cruise around in his little Falcon. This day he was fidgeting at the radio dial as we drove. Then he relaxed after hitting on what to me was a unique and splendid sound. This, he announced, was a group called the Beatles. "You gotta hear it!"

THE FIRST TRI: AS A YOUNG MAN

But keep in mind, no radios at Borromeo. After that weekend, we all had the same idea. Had to hear more. Out came tiny transistor radios, earphones, and, in desperation, homemade crystal sets.

Perhaps I too was getting caught up in the idea of change. My dream to become a parish priest was fading a bit, and I was considering moving to an order of missionaries, in this case the Glendale order who focused their efforts on Appalachia and our rural south. I had a very good friend in the seminary, Denny McDonnell, who had the same idea. Denny had come in from St. Joe's High School after distinguishing himself as a scholar and a wrestler. He and I spent a lot of time together in class, on the field or walking the quadrangle and hills of the campus. If you had told us in 1964 that, #1 neither of you will become priests, and #2 your daughters will marry each other sixty years from now, we would consider the teller of such a story simply delusional. Ah, how time changes us.

I took a Red Cross life-saving course when the seminary opened the pool in the spring. As graduation approached, we were filled with both excitement and not a little trepidation. Classmates, who had bravely flaunted the rules over the years and were now on their way out, were positively weepy in our closing days.

Does anyone really remember his high school graduation? I am sure mine was gloriously formal and just right for the day. Denny and I would be going to St. Gregory's Seminary in Cincinnati in the fall. Others were moving in different directions, and half the class would matriculate to Borromeo College. But a lovely long summer stretched out in front of us for now.

CHAPTER 7

The summer of 1965 marked the opening of Willoughby's new swimming pool complex. The old dam was now closed, and only a few years ago from this writing was ruptured by a flood and removed entirely. The new pool was built on Euclid Avenue a little west of town, close to the police and fire stations, just in front of the high school. Now I was a senior life-saver and must have just slid into that job at the new pool. There were fifteen to twenty of us, all about 17-20 years old. (As a footnote: In the summers of more recent times our city pools have been unable to maintain regular hours because there are not enough young people getting that Red Cross certificate and taking life-guarding jobs. Or maybe they have found other things to do.)

The crew met for orientation in the basement of city hall, a week or so after graduation. I knew a number of them already from playing sandlot baseball well into my teens. Among the group was my old friend Rick Uritus and Carol McLaughlin, the lifeguard from the kiddie pool of last summer at Daniels Park. Carol and I had exchanged a couple letters in my senior year at Borromeo which I read late at night with a flashlight, when I was a prefect in the freshman Hoban Hall. It was nice to see her among this fresh lot of co-workers.

The work at the pool was not much work. It involved sitting high up on one of four stands around the pool, watching the kids and adults swimming below in different sections of the large pool. We had a ten-minute break every hour. That's when we could get a snack, socialize or get in the water to add to our quarter mile that lifeguards were expected to swim every day. The most interesting of the guard stands was the one adjacent to the two diving boards, one meter and three meters off the water. Not too many swimmers had any idea how to dive, but way too many tried, usually feet first or in a loud belly-flop. We had to be a little more on our toes up there, and have a towel ready for those "failures of costumes," especially with the girls in two-piece suits. Did I even think about Monsignor Whalen and his kindly advice four years earlier to "avoid mixed company?" To me, this was happily ground zero.

Most of the lifeguards and others working around the pool had gone to South High, just over there. And each of them had friends who also came to the pool. There was much talk about who was going with whom, sad tales of senior break-ups, talk of college plans, and references to last year's big games. Not much to do with me. Perhaps I was something of an anomaly to them: very much a part the group, equally apart from the group. A few who didn't know me very well pretended to watch their language in my presence, or made indecipherable comments that suggested a slight discomfort.

But actually, I was well-embedded in the pool group, and many days we would make plans to go out after work to the "Torchlight," a big dance hall that served 3/2 beer, i.e. 3.2 percent alcohol which was legal for eighteen-year-olds. Some nights I would drive out to Painesville, the county seat, with another lifeguard to become a Water Safety Instructor. This made me a certified teacher of all levels of swimming, including lifesaving.

Often our parents would deliver our dinners to the pool when we were on duty and this would arouse the curiosity and hunger of our fellow guards. On one such occasion my friend Jeff grabbed a fork and stuffed in a mouthful of salad, just delivered by my brother, at exactly the same moment the phone rang in the manager's office. My mother was screaming at the other end. "Don't touch the salad!" And simultaneously Jeff was spitting his out. My mother had inadvertently (Jeff questioned that.) mixed up the salad vinegar with ammonia. I still see Jeff now and again, and he hasn't forgotten.

It was a good job that summer and a lot of fun. But that's not at all what made it a most significant time of my life. I fell in love with the girl named Carol. I think there's a line from "Our Town" where the narrator says something like, "Who can say how these things start?" I was blinded and dumbstruck, so don't ask me. We picked up our conversations where we left off the summer before, and we began to walk home together, since we both lived close to town. Our walks took longer and longer door to door, because we had found a stopping off point, perched up by the water tower overlooking the Chagrin valley.

It was pretty obvious what this all meant, but I'm a slow learner. The seminary at St. Gregory's in Cincinnati was scheduled to open in late-August, and I was committed to go. But the leaving produced a sickening sadness deep within. The long summer of '65 was no longer.

St. Gregory's in Cincinnati

CHAPTER 8

St. Gregory's Seminary, newly accredited as the "Atheneum of Ohio," was a formidable 19th century German gothic structure high above the Ohio River. It was a diocesan seminary, like Borromeo, but the Glendale order that I signed on to trained their aspiring priests there as well. Many of the large group of seminarians in my new class had come up through their minor seminary, so they had their own bundle of common stories, school legends and folkways. My roommate was Paul, good-looking and a brilliant scholar, who also did his high school years at the seminary. And, he was a very nice guy.

Looking down or onto the next page, you will see that this is a relatively short chapter in my life. You can guess why. I was sick, but not for home. My friend Denny was at the seminary too, and we spent a lot of time walking the campus and talking, or not.

Every seminarian was assigned a spiritual adviser coming in. I have no recollection of who my adviser was, but I sought out his help in getting through this. After listening to my saga, which I kept to a bare-bones minimum, the good father suggested I divide a sheet of paper in two and write all the reasons I wanted to stay and all the reasons I wanted to leave on each side, and bring it back to him. I did half of what he asked. I wrote out the sheet, looked at the two columns, then called my parents to come pick me up the next day.

CHAPTER 9

On the ride home with my dad he let me know that the nest was no longer empty. In the month that I was gone, my thirteen-year-old cousin and her pregnant sixteen-year-old sister had moved in. That's the way it was done in those days. You get pregnant, you leave town for a while, have a baby who will be adopted by a good Catholic family and return home looking like any other healthy girl of now seventeen. Sadly, I saw that my cousin from the east coast was still very much in love and desperate to stay in touch with her young lover. The thirteen-year-old sister was enjoying the emotional circus swirling around her. My mother and her broken dreams of my becoming a priest added their own weight to the tangible distress of the household.

So I'm home. Now what? I had never applied to a college, hadn't taken or even heard of an SAT, and the only surety I had to cling to was that I was moving in the right direction, no going back. My uncle, my mother's brother, suddenly came on the scene and did something of a deus ex machina. He happened to be on the board of John Carroll University or at least was on friendly enough terms with the president there that he arranged a meeting the next day with the three of us.

This was already the first of week of October and class had been in session for two weeks because of the JCU semester calendar. Years later, when I was teaching a freshman college course, a new student in the front row appeared nervous and unsettled. He stayed after class and confided that he had never gone to a school outside of his father's military base camps. This was his first day, and I knew exactly how he felt. After it was quickly agreed that I could begin school, even two weeks late, my uncle departed, a schedule was created, and down the administrative hall I went. First to the bookstore where I bought a heavy pile of college textbooks, then to the R.O.T.C. building to get my required uniform, and finally, I think, to a class or two in the afternoon, lugging it all with me. Oh dear, what have I gotten myself into? College, son.

My parents knew nothing about Carol, and I had no idea how to get in touch with her. She was already into her own new life as a freshman at Oberlin College, and I wasn't even sure how she would respond to my early exit and sudden dropping out of the blue. We had a mutual friend, Jeff of ammonia salad-eating fame, who was also at Oberlin, so I worked out an overnight there in his dorm and reunited with Carol. Her own dorm was a carefully guarded buttress of all women, in Oberlin's last year of all-women dorms. When frequently asked at her reunions through the years if I too had gone to Oberlin, my response has to be, "Only on weekends." That fall Carol and I traveled back and forth whenever we could. Life in college can be very consuming, and we were both committed to our studies, so it wasn't as if I was about to sweep Carol away. However, I'm guessing it was that autumn that I proposed to her for the first of many times.

Life at home in Willoughby was a little chaotic. Many nights I'd walk into town with my sixteen-year-old cousin so she could dump a pile of change into the public telephone in front of the library and spend a minute talking to the father of her growing baby. I worked part time guarding a local hotel pool in the evenings and deposited quite a number of my own quarters trying to catch Carol at the house phone in her dorm. That didn't leave a lot of time to attend to my nineteen-hour college schedule. My parents were simply trying to figure out who all these people were, including me, and who was this girl, a non-Catholic named Carol.

Things changed after the new year. My cousins left us to go "somewhere else." That's all I heard, for the baby's birth. I lived at home for the rest of the school year, but must have been too busy with study and work to remember any details.

In retrospect, this time at home must have involved considerable readjustment. I had been away for the entirety of high-school and now was home, for awhile. But home was the easy part. Outside, at the university, at work, my horizons were expanding every day.

CHAPTER 10

*I*n my first year at John Carroll, I had a very young and vibrant English instructor named Sherri O'Donnell who made an enormous impression and shook up, if not punctured the bubble that I had been living in. She pored over my writing and made incisive comments and suggestions. She invited me and others to faculty and teaching-assistant gatherings, where everyone's opinion was highly valued. The world I came from had been sharply divided between students and teachers, adults and children. I had crossed over or maybe those walls in 1965-1966 were shifting if not coming down. But what had the most effect on me in those days was Miss O'Donnell's vehement anti-war stance. Her position was compelling, at polar opposites of what I had heard from other adults in my life, and this teacher went far to help me broaden and clarify my own thinking.

I must have been living at home all of that first college year because I well-remember my summer job that followed. Tucked behind a couple of those lovely homes on Euclid Avenue was a small factory,

Willo-Hill Industries, that produced small steel components for unnamed, industrial application. There were basically three groups of us on the floor, excepting the owner and foreman. The toolmakers and machinists were newly arrived immigrants from eastern Europe, smart, willing to work for small wages, and unable to speak English. A second group came mostly from the south, especially Appalachia, and lived in the trailer parks scattered about the county. They worked hard for their low pay, but the scuttlebutt about trailer-park life helped to explain their higher absenteeism and job turnover. The rest of us, fewer in number, were college students, eyes wide open, and probably aspiring to a different future. Piecework is what they call it, sitting at a punch-press, or a drilling or a deburring machine, and moving pieces from one bin to another. I don't remember the pay, and would be embarrassed by the number even if adjusted for inflation. What I do remember was that we worked ten hours a day and eight on Saturday. Fifty-eight hours a week without overtime. It was exhausting and left little time for my social or any other kind of life. Didn't see much of the sun that summer either. And if that wasn't bad enough, I realized later that some of those cannisters that I was de-burring would soon be filled with explosives in some other factory and sent to Vietnam. Not so romantic a story as the summer before.

Toward the fall, now going into my second year of college, I was invited to join the staff of child care workers at St. Anthony's Home for Boys on the west side of Cleveland. The home housed high school students who had aged out of the Parmadale orphanage. I had a room there (my first room to myself), but it was probably more akin to Fr. Murphy's spartan aesthetic than to a modern teen's pleasure dome. Two other John Carroll students were already working there and the three of us commuted across town together to John Carroll. Monsignor Ciolek, the head of Catholic Charities of the diocese, also lived there and was in charge of St. Anthony's.

The next couple years, I lived by the study habits I had adopted in the seminary. I signed up for early morning classes as much as I was able, had lunch in the student center with old friends and new, then sequestered myself at a corner carillon in the library and studied in the afternoon until it was time to drive or catch a ride back across town to work. We tried to make St. Anthony's a home. But three college men and a gruff old cleric are not the stuff of hominess for a group of forty-five male high school residents, each with his own complicated personal history. Our work was mostly about keeping schedules and keeping order, some tutoring, and contributing to a log detailing boys' behaviors and their responses for their social workers who came and went. The boys were not entirely confined to the home: they attended any of four or five different local high schools and were free to come and go, as long they checked in and showed up for meals, study periods, and bed. A few of the boys were actually older than I was at nineteen, but to all of them I was "Mr. Fishwick."

St. Anthony's Home was closer to Oberlin, and I continued to find time to make the drive out in my yellow Comet to see Carol there. But I had my work and studies, and Carol was immersed in her own studies and a campus life I could only dream of. Closer to Oberlin I was, but with the feeling that the distance was growing slightly if not steadily.

In April of my second year at John Carroll, my father, fifty years old, passed away rather suddenly. He had been plagued his whole adult life with heart issues, and it didn't help that he smoked two or three packs of cigarettes a day. He spent a week in the hospital which should have alarmed me more than it did. And that was it.

In the weeks or months before my father died, he had again taken up the trumpet which he had played in high school. On the morning after he died, my mother insisted that I return the borrowed trumpet to Arrowhead Music. I suppose she associated his playing with his demise. In the store that morning was a kindly clerk, round of face with a big smile. I told him who I was and that I wished to return the instrument. He looked shocked. I think he and my father had had some friendly exchanges and he was confused that I was returning the horn. "What happened?" he asked. "Anything wrong with it?" I stood there, frozen, welling up inside. "No," I bawled, "My dad died last night," and left in a flood.

A week before my father went into the hospital, he had been painting closets. Yeah, I know, who paints closets? Well, Paul did, and I can imagine him inside one of those two by four spaces, a Kent ("with the micronite filter") hanging from his lips while he rolled the paint on. Whew!

My older brothers were married now and had their own homes. Younger brother Bob was still in the seminary, so it seemed obvious that I would need to leave St. Anthony's and move home again for a while. I was back in class at John Carroll the next week, and I'm sure my grades took something of a hit that semester.

In the summer, while living at home with my mother, I joined a grade-school friend, Tom Brigham, in the first of several summers painting houses. Tom's mother worked in real-estate. She recommended to clients on occasion that the house they hoped to sell would be more marketable with a fresh coat of paint, and didn't she just have a son who could make that happen. We worked hard, but no one would confuse us with professional painters. Carol was spending the summer with her Oberlin roommate in Turkey and Austria, so, while the work was certainly better than the deburring machine at Willo-Hill Industries last year, my social life didn't improve much.

CHAPTER 11

*M*y mother by this time, late summer, was getting on her feet, and I was getting in her way. Tom and I may have run out of painting jobs, or maybe we ran out of energy. In any event, in early August I stuck out my thumb and headed to Montreal for Expo '67, which did much to clear my head. I had hitchhiked before, mostly around town, but this was the first long trip I took with many to follow. I reckoned at one point that I had traversed in those years the equivalent of the globe's circumference. Hard to imagine now, entrusting one's travel and life in the hands of a stranger passing by in truck or car.

Several things stand out in my memory of that trip to Montreal and beyond, the least of which was probably the exposition itself. A hotel there would have been way too expensive and I wasn't nearly sophisticated enough to have made such plans. So I am guessing there was a youth hostel set up as part of Expo accommodations. I do remember meeting a young French student, wherever it was we stayed, and we traveled together for a few days. On August

15th, the feast of the Assumption, he and I agreed to attend mass in Montreal for the holy day. The reason this stands out is that it may have been the last time I made the decision to go to mass as a practicing Catholic. Of course, I have attended many masses at weddings and funerals since, and I took my mother to midnight mass every Christmas. But without any lightning, crisis of faith, or anything negative at all to precipitate, I had, as my mother would say, "fallen away."

The little bit of French I took in college was still reasonably fresh, and it was exciting to actually depend on it when I went on to Quebec where I explored the old city and a bit of night life. From Quebec I hitched down to Lake George, New York, to visit a friend who was employed at a summer resort. Life was easy there, young and old were having a great time. Good to kick back for a few days. One of the people I befriended, Cathy, was a precocious young adolescent who quizzed me about everything I read or had studied or thought about life, art and literature. Innocent enough. Keep her in mind. I was soon on my way.

Next stop was New York City, LaGuardia I think, where I met Carol coming home from her summer abroad. She was probably exhausted from travel, and her luggage was full of memories and mementos that she was anxious to share with her family back in Willoughby. Our meeting and night in New York was uneventful. It was as if we were now speaking two different languages, more figuratively than literally, but indeed Carol had been using her German quite extensively in Austria. She flew home the next day, and I hitched out through the Lincoln Tunnel on my way to Washington, D.C.

Pat Reymann was a very good high school friend of mine. He was charming and charmed, a brilliant student at Georgetown who aspired first to the Foreign Service, but later chose to go to Stanford Law School. That summer he had been housesitting for a well-to-do family who was travelling. We had only a couple days together because he was packing to spend a semester in Germany himself. He had to leave, but he gave me the keys to this Georgetown palais, and I spent another night. The next day I finally headed west to Ohio.

CHAPTER 12

Sometime before the start of the new semester of my third year at John Carroll, I got a call from Monsignor Ciolek, my boss from St. Anthony's Home and the head of Catholic Charities. The diocese had acquired the former seminary of the Blessed Sacrament Order on Euclid Avenue at around East 152nd. Don Bosco, as it was called, had been vacant for a while, and there was concern that the place was being vandalized. The monsignor asked if I could live there and watch over the buildings and grounds. For me it was a straight shot up Belvoir to John Carroll, close enough to bicycle on occasion. Don Bosco was a three-story building sitting on a hill above Euclid Avenue. The upper two floors were dorm rooms, maybe fifteen rooms on each floor. The first floor comprised the chapel, sacristy, and what were probably two larger priest's quarters. Out back, or through an underground tunnel if you wished to go that way, was the gymnasium/dining hall with a large kitchen on one side. Several acres of playing fields made up the rest of the campus. It was an unusual offer that I couldn't refuse.

I asked my friend, Denny McDonnell, who had left the seminary not long after I had and was now a student at Cleveland State, if he'd like to join me "on the hill." He took one of the rooms on the first floor; I took a room at the top of the stairs on the second. And that left a lot of rooms. Denny brought his dog Lance, a German shepherd mix, which proved to be all the protection we would need.

My study habits didn't change. I continued to sign up for early morning classes and then study in the library in the afternoons. Throughout my college career I carried courseloads of twenty hour credits each semester, and this would factor in to a later decision. Some evenings and weekends I worked at a large grocery store between school and the hill, packing bags and cleaning up. The job was quite forgettable, but I mention it along with the factory work, house-painting, child-care work to make the point of how far away I was from college campus life. There was no one from home paying the bills, but I was lucky to go to school at a time when tuition would not strap me with years of student debt. Tuition was thirty dollars per credit hour, so per semester the bill was six hundred dollars. Denny and I ate a lot of chicken pot pies at Don Bosco, six for a dollar, and had a palace in which to live like kings.

Our place on the hill soon became something of a mecca. Friends from John Carroll and Cleveland State, friends of friends and old acquaintances from other colleges came to Don Bosco. We had parties on the roof overlooking the east side and Lake Erie, seances in the chapel, murals painted on the walls, and endless nights in the living room/sacristy listening to music and solving world problems. We never knew from day to day who was coming or going. Dorm life on campus couldn't have been this heady.

One evening in the darkening days of late fall, Cathy Lawless, the young girl I had met at Lake George and with whom I had exchanged a couple of letters, came calling at the door. She had taken a bus from Buffalo and joined the party, you might say, which turned out to be short-lived. At about eleven o'clock that night our place on the hill was surrounded by six to eight cop cars, lights on, radios blaring. What we had not known was that teenager Cathy's father was on the supreme court of New York state, and you might say he was well-connected. I knew her age, and knew enough to step aside when the storm troopers burst on the scene. She was whisked away, but the story of Cathy Lawless was just beginning.

American society early in 1968 was coming apart at the seams. Anger in the inner cities was flaring into flames; protests over U.S. involvement in Vietnam were turning violent; family gatherings dissolving into vicious arguments. In early spring, March I think, Martin Luther King, Jr. was assassinated. In June, while I was painting Denny's mother's house and listening to the radio, the program was interrupted to announce that young Bobby Kennedy, the most likely presidential candidate for the Democratic Party, was also gunned down.

My regular trips to Oberlin College became fewer in that year and then not at all. Carol was moving on and apart, and when I did seek her out, she would not be found. If I asked at her dorm if she was there, the cryptic responses made things very clear. "No, haven't seen Carol in a while, but Wayne was just here a few minutes ago." As if I was looking for Wayne.

Something had to change. I was desperate for change. The prospect of reading literature and philosophy for another year as a senior, then doing student teaching and being drafted into the army looked bleak and lonely. Unimaginable, really. At some point in the spring of my third year, I added up the number of credit hours I had completed. It turned out that I was only a few hours short of graduation because of my courseload over the last three years. I could complete the requirements with some summer work and graduate in August. With that information I applied to the Peace Corps. I got the work done over the summer and threw a graduation party for myself in late August.

CHAPTER 13

*A*fter the requisite security checks and health clearance, the Peace Corps accepted me as a teacher in secondary school and told me I would be going to Liberia, West Africa. The first step would be teacher training in Durham, North Carolina, beginning in late October. That would give me more than a month to try my hand at substitute teaching in Cleveland's inner city. There is probably a story a day to tell about that experience, but what stands out was my very first day.

Substitute teachers are called around six in the morning. I know because I had to make those calls myself in my later teaching career. Teaching colleagues would call me first, and then I spent the next half hour or so trying to find a willing sub. My assignment that mid-September day was East High School, close to downtown Cleveland. I pulled in just before eight. It didn't seem as though I was to be filling in for a specific teacher, and it soon became apparent that I was among a vast herd of substitute teachers who were asked to report to the gym. There we were told that a teacher had been accosted outside the school the day before. Security was a major concern, and the entire teaching staff walked out in solidarity over the issue. The principal explained that he wanted to keep the school open, both for the safety of the students and to convince the hungry press that…that what? That it was no big deal?

We were each assigned a classroom, probably organized by homeroom not related to a specific course area. Our job was to teach, entertain, or do whatever was possible to keep these high school students in one room, so that from the outside there would be some semblance of a normal school day. It wasn't normal, and I felt like a scab. The kids treated me well and we had a reasonably good time. For a while. But it was a balmy late summer day, the windows were open, and we were on the first floor. By early afternoon a number of the more rambunctious had bailed, jumped out the window. And who was I to stop them? The ones left behind were the readers, the quiet talkers, the ones who remembered the deck of cards they had stashed among their books. That was my first day as a paid teacher, and I earned it.

Durham, North Carolina, was chosen as the location of teacher training, not because it was the home of Duke University, quite the opposite. The city itself was depressed and unbalanced, and there were boycotts of merchants slow to throw off Jim Crow and sit-ins at lunch counters. I lived with a Black family, James and Faye and their two boys, Troy and Donahue. Really. They were gentle, soft-spoken people whom I came to greatly admire. James worked late nights cleaning a local movie theater. I joined him on occasion. We ate a lot of popcorn. The teacher-training itself was excellent, carried out by the education department of Greensborough A & T, an historically Black college. Classes were conducted at Hillsboro High School, halfway between Durham and Greensborough, where we also did a condensed version of student teaching. It was every bit as good as what I missed by absconding before my senior year of college. We each went back home for Christmas and prepared to fly to West Africa before the new year.

Two or three days after Christmas, on the night before I was to leave, there was a knock at the side door of our house on Park Avenue. It was Carol whom I had not seen since sometime over the summer. Not much to say as we stood in the vestibule next to the washer and dryer machines. She was in the middle of her last year at Oberlin, home for the holidays. We embraced and said goodbye, neither of us with any idea of what the future held. I flew out the next morning.

CHAPTER 14

We took a chartered flight out of New York, refueled in Madrid. Our training group from Durham was joined by another group of volunteers who had trained for other roles than secondary teaching. This group had trained in the Virgin Islands. Yeah, I know, Durham/Virgin Islands, I felt the same way. Together we were surely a much larger contingent than was the norm, but, as the first batch of baby boomers, you might say we were getting used to bigger crowds.

Liberia is/was an anomaly, situated between the former British colony of Sierra Leone and the French colony of Ivory Coast. In fact, it is a rare African state that was never a colony. But it was certainly colonized. In the early 1800s U.S. presidents Madison and Monroe, among many other politicians, abolitionists and slaveholders, took up the idea of re-patriating Black freemen and freed slaves to Africa. Each group had their own motives in this plan. When I arrived in the late 1960s the government, politics and economics of the country were still controlled by the descendants of those early settlers who came on boats from America more than a hundred years before. Americo-Liberians, as they are called, settled mostly along the coast and comprise less than ten percent of the population. They created by law a Black republic. The rest of the population consisted of more than two dozen indigenous groups, each with their own language. Much has changed in fifty years since I was there, so I can only hope that those languages are still heard, the stories still told, and the diverse groups able to hold on to their distinct native cultures.

English is the national language, Liberians have a flag and a constitution modeled after the U.S., and the U.S. dollar is their currency. In some ways Americo-Liberian fashion, their official ceremonies, and even their distinctive English language was frozen in time around 1840-1850. The sad irony is that the early founders, having lived in the United States, set themselves up in the same way as what they had experienced in their days of bondage. Now they could be plantation owners; now they could make slaves of the indigenous people. And they did. The League of Nations reported in the 1930s that Liberia was the last nation in the world with officially sanctioned slavery.

That's a little background. Some of it I probably learned at our first stop in Kakata, not far from Robertsfield, the airport where we landed. Orientation was brief. I celebrated my twenty-second birthday on New Year's Eve in Kakata, and within days the whole lot of us were scattered across the country to the areas of our posts for language studies. A small group of us went to Buchanan, named after the first governor of the republic (1839-1841) and a relative of U.S. President James Buchanan. It was a sleepy coastal town about a hundred miles from the capital of Monrovia, of course named after the author of the Monroe Doctrine which gave permission for America to stretch from sea to sea and beyond because it was our manifest destiny.

The language of the indigenous people along that part of the coast was Bassa. It was highly tonal and had a lovely sound when spoken, but the city of Buchanan was uncharacteristically cosmopolitan and not even the majority there spoke Bassa. Various tribal groups lived in small communities around town: Fanti fishermen from Ghana lived close to the beach; the Vai were Mande Muslims from the west; the Kru were a strong presence from the east of Liberia; Americo-Liberians held office. Then there were the Lebanese merchants who bought and sold anything bigger than what you could find in the markets or the smaller stores of the Mandingos. Just east of town was a gated community of Swedes who lived apart, quite insulated, and co-owned the Liberian-American Mining Company. Buchanan was the coastal port with a smelting factory for iron-ore that was brought in on rail from Nimba, a county in the hills, far interior. Then there were the ships and sailors docking regularly to transport the ore out. Buchanan was to me a very exciting place to live for the next two years, but learning Bassa in six weeks from a Bassa man who had never taught was not the stuff of focused academia. Just too many things to get my attention in those early days.

Going to school or shopping in the market, I could greet people along the way in Bassa, the outer limits of my language skills. One day I bought a pair of clear-plastic sandals at the outdoor

Liberian American Mining Company smelting plant

market, around the "corner" from where I lived and was wearing them proudly. As I walked down the street, I could see that the ladies along the side were chuckling and pointing, "Gbwe se nini dyi" they called. "Gbwe se nini dyi" they giggled in Bassa. I was walking with one of my students who seemed to be caught up in the joke himself. "What's going on, Stephen," I asked. "What does 'gbwe se nini dyi' mean? "It means," he said, "a dog doesn't eat his own shit." I still wasn't getting it. "Yeah, well, so what does that mean?" Stephen laughed in his endearing way and simply said, "Look at the bottom of your shoes." Those plastic sandals were locally notorious, with their spiky soles, for picking up any and all roadside detritus. That may be the only Bassa I've retained, except for the unfortunate label most white people were tagged with, "Wudi pu gah." Man with money.

After our language training we were now distributed through the Bassa county to our posts. Some of my fellow volunteers went to walk-in villages deep in the forest, others to places along the road to Monrovia. I remained in Buchanan and would be teaching at St. Peter Claver Catholic missionary school, a large and well-established grade school of several hundred students. The opening of school was the first of March and would go through the rainy season until November. Although we received a small stipend for our housing, volunteers were expected to find their own place and negotiate the rent. I found a place with a volunteer from New York named Richard, but that didn't work out in the long run. Richard was an example among many, of a volunteer whose job was not very clearly defined. He taught in the high school, but it was never clear to me (or him, I think) exactly what he was supposed to teach or what his hours were. He languished in a cloud of weed and left the country when he could. Other volunteers who worked in public works projects or some type of community services suffered from the same confusion and ultimate malaise or departure.

I taught school, simple as that. Seventh and eighth grade, English, math, science. The two classes were large, vibrant and an amazing cross-section of young people from the surrounding area. I wore a tie every day, got there early, taught and socialized, and read papers at night. Nothing confusing about my expectations of myself and my students.

St. Peter Claver was run by Father Korfant, from somewhere in eastern Europe, for whom his Jesuit order had probably run out of ideas. He did not hold Africans in high esteem, and for that reason, after my first half year teaching, he made the embarrassing request that I become principal of the school while he was on leave in the second half of the school year. He had set the poor example of cancelling school if it happened to be raining in the morning. You need to know that the coast of Liberia gets an incredible 180 inches of rain in the six-month rainy season, which coincides with the school year. If he put one of his African staff in charge he expected a lot of in-fighting and not much day-to-day school because of weather. I was twenty-two years old, not old enough to say no, and if my primary duty was to either hold class or cancel school, I would say we put in many more days in that second semester than we did before Father Korfant took leave.

With Stephen Gray at the house near market

But if that makes me sound somewhat tyrannical, I should point out that the school day ended just after noon each day. On nice days I'd head to the beach, a hundred miles of mostly deserted sand. Africans weren't swimmers. I suppose too many had been swept out to sea, which was mostly attributed to the evil water spirits who lived below the surf. You might find a few very noticeable (because very white) Swedes on the beach, the only time they seemed to emerge from their compound. Otherwise, the long stretch was ours. A later roommate was a blond kid from California named Jack, a real beach boy who rode a motorcycle and taught me to spearfish for red snapper. Not a bad life.

The ocean drops off to the deep quickly along that coast, and one incident early on gave me a very serious perspective on the dangers lurking. A young Peace Corps couple had come for a visit from an up-country post, and of course we went to the beach. The three of us were treading water not far from shore, talking and not paying attention. But we were drifting apart. Within minutes the man was a good fifty feet away and moving further out. His wife headed to the shore, and I realized that I would have to go out and bring him in. My years of lifeguarding around a pool hadn't prepared me for this. I had never saved anyone, though I might have extended a pole to some kid who belly-flopped hard off the high dive. The rest of the story that day is about adrenalin. My friend was pretty tired out by the time I swam out to him, even though it had only been a matter of minutes. I threw my arm across his chest and side-stroked against the ripping tide. The swim back took a long time and we were both exhausted when we washed up on the beach, laughing and crying at the same time.

During the worst of the rainy season, when torrents came pounding on the corrugated steel roof, I read books or entertained a steady flow of students coming and going. The Peace Corps issued each of us a cardboard book locker with two shelves crammed with popular novels of the day. There were three different sets, so when you finished one, you would trade yours with another volunteer, and start on set number two.

And then there was the nightlife. The sailors—Russians, Taiwanese, Venezuelans—came in from the ships for a good time at the few bars in Buchanan. Otis Redding seemed always to be on the jukebox, "sittin' on the dock of the bay." And the movie theater in town a short distance from the ocean played spaghetti westerns and Hitchcock's "The Birds" frequently enough for me to mumble the lines in my sleep.

The Africans went wild over everything they saw at the cinema, and I came to understand why one day in one of my classes. A fairly bright student asked how the filmmakers could know there was going to be a fight when they took their equipment into a bar or out on the plains. Uh oh, I thought, this isn't a case of suspended disbelief. They are taking it for real. So, over the next week, without a movie camera, we wrote out scripts, cleared the front of the classroom, and acted out scenes which we pretended to capture on film for our non-production. Actually, a Liberian's understanding of film probably wasn't too far removed from the crowd I later saw in Cleveland who stood and wildly cheered at the smashing victory of "Rocky" (I, II or III?).

Toward the end of my first year of teaching and the end of rainy season, I received a letter from Carol saying she'd like to come to Liberia over the holidays, one year since I had seen her at our farewell next to the washing machine. It was a wonderful and romantic reunion. We tried to see it all or none of it, depending on the day. The beach, the movies, the market, my curious students, my quirky little house with its screaming frogs out the back door, and the way too shallow well in the front. Her departure after the new year left a gaping hole, but this time I knew we would see each other again.

Out of Africa

CHAPTER 15

Something about travel and one's utter focus on getting there and getting around works to allay or at least postpone our attention to feelings of loss or to such "gaping holes" of the heart. In early January, I joined a large group of volunteers who flew together to East Africa—Kenya, Uganda, and Tanzania. We all split up in Nairobi with our own itineraries and went off for a month of travel. My mode of transportation was, of course, a trusty thumb. I set out for Kampala, Uganda. I wish now that I could remember all the rides and the people I met along the way. They were generous, informative, full of personal stories, and on many occasions gave me a place to stay overnight.

One was a professor at the University of Nairobi who loved going out to photograph a family of cheetahs that he seemed to know by name. He carried a tub of sliced carrots in the back seat which we helped ourselves to like popcorn. The cheetahs seemed to know him, too, because once we were parked, a couple cats jumped onto the car roof and lolled about while my companion took pictures from inside the car. As we were later driving away, he spotted a female lion carrying its prey, presumably to her cubs. He wanted to get a better look, and off we went over the plains until we caught up and were close enough to see mama feeding her family, and none of them paying any attention to us. Up to a point. When we had seen enough and it as time to go, the professor put the car in gear and… spun the wheels. We were up on a boulder and rubber was not meeting the road, so to speak. I would have to get out and rock the car, my back to the lion and her cubs. She didn't like that. Well, I didn't either. She roared her displeasure and made a move in my direction. At that point I probably had the strength to throw the car in the air. I smacked my head jumping back in and we went with a lurch. The professor had taken six rolls of thirty-six exposures that day, and said he was worried about what his wife would say because he had taken just as many shots the day before. I had a few more carrots before he dropped me off.

In the days before Idi Amin, Kampala, Uganda was a beautiful and verdant city on the north end of Lake Victoria. From Kampala I must have back-tracked a bit when I headed to Serengeti, the massive preserve in Tanzania and home to large herds of all the iconic beasts of African lore. I got a ride from two nuns heading in that direction. They left me on the edge of the park where I thought I could get a ride. It was a dusty dirt road, and no cars came or went. Eventually, as I was considering the prospect of spending the night in the bush, one car did come along and stopped. Two young Tanzanian guys told me that they may be the last car coming down this road in days. They also said it would be akin to suicide for me to sleep outside anywhere in the region—I'd be gobbled up (my words). They invited me to stay the night at their house not too far away. One of them was a veterinarian, the other a nurse at a health clinic. What an impressive pair they were, enough to give me pause in thinking about my teaching in West Africa. Julius Nyerere was the president of Tanzania at the time and was fiercely anti-colonial. He wanted the countryside to be well-educated and well-served, so that the people would not all clamor to find a place in the capital of Dar-es-Salaam. These two young men I was staying with were part of that dream of social and local progress. My students in Liberia saw success as a desk job in Monrovia, the capital. Their aspirations were about individual success and a degree of wealth. That's not a criticism of the many students I had come to know and whose company I so much enjoyed. It was endemic to their world. The idea of society rising together was not part of that scheme. I would have to think about this more and consider what part I play as a teacher.

On I went. Across the Serengeti, to Ngorongoro Crater, up close to Kilimanjaro (But I didn't take the time to climb.). On to Dar-es-Salaam and a small plane to Zanzibar, the island of spices. The last stop before returning to Nairobi was Mombasa and its beautiful sandy beaches on the Indian Ocean. Looking back on my trip to East Africa, I can't say how much of it bears any semblance to what I would find there today or how I would travel. It was good for me and a much-expanded version of my month hitching to Expo and down the east coast a couple years before.

CHAPTER 16

*M*y two-year stint in Africa seemed to take on a pattern similar to that of classical drama: introduction, rising action, climax, falling action, denouement. The climax were those two marvelous months just described between the school terms. In the second year I experienced, maybe not falling, but a loosening of the exciting grip Africa had on me. Teaching was becoming routine, Father Korfant was replaced by a strapping young Irish priest who left no doubt as to who was in charge, and for me and many others our attentions were turning toward what comes next.

The Vietnam War was still raging. Nixon's secret plan to end the war after getting elected was to bomb Cambodia to oblivion. Didn't work out. More troops were needed and the youth were getting wise. During those so-called "marvelous months" that I was enjoying, the selective service (what a name) devised a draft lottery. Into a barrel went three hundred sixty-six birthdays, and these were drawn out one by one to see who went first. A number of my fellow volunteers huddled around a short-wave radio at the post office and listened for the news of their number. My New Year's Eve birthday came up #5. Others, whose numbers were in the two or three hundreds, started packing up to go home. These were volunteers who hadn't been too sure about why they were there in the first place, and now a considerable obstacle in their path had been cleared. I liked teaching at St. Peter's and figured the chips would fall for me somewhere down my own road.

I was very close to a few students who seemed to be part of the household, and I remember three of them well, their names and faces vividly—Augustus Jaeploe, George Gbeah, and Stephen Gray. They came from different indigenous tribal groups, and probably didn't know each other well. But they certainly knew me. On the other hand, the adults I was acquainted with, whether they were fellow teachers, local politicians, or the man selling meat in the market, seemed so distant in their worldview that it was difficult to engage in any conversation that went deeper than greetings or commerce. Once I met a young Liberian who had studied at Ohio State, obviously far outside any usual educational track, like the ones that prepared you for a desk job in Monrovia. He knew Liberia, but his understanding of the world was so much broader that I wondered how he ever fit back in to Liberian society. Our meeting was brief, but here was a man whom I could imagine being good friends with.

The house I lived in was built and owned by a Mandingo chief named Homadu Jallah. He also served as the local judge for any of the palavers (a common word in Liberia) that came up between offending parties. He was noted to give wise counsel. As I mentioned, it was up to Peace Corps volunteers to negotiate their own rents. One day I heard that Homadu Jallah was hoping to raise my rent and was on his way over. The chief always walked with a retinue of his Mandingo assistants, tall and robed, formidable as they walked behind Homadu. I had to think fast because I knew the chief would not get any more money from local renters than he could get from me and the Peace Corps. I stopped him in his tracks before he and his entourage reached the front door, and said, "Very good to see you, Mr. Jallah. I was hoping to see you today to discuss the rent. You see, I think I'm paying you too much." He took the bait, and in the next few minutes explained why he thought what I was paying was the right amount. I demurred and finally agreed that he made a good case. The rent would stay the same. Is that what they call a win-win?

There is so much more to say about Liberia, the American friends I made, the endless jamming on guitars and long nights talking about books and listening to whatever new music was making the scene (about six months late). "Abbey Road" and "The Band" blew us away; James Taylor gave us Joni Mitchell and more. Foreign visitors were dropped off at my house because the taxis knew a Peace Corps man lived there, close to the market. A young German making his way across West Africa by himself. Black American men looking for their roots. My students could recognize them as foreign from a long way off. They observed keenly and just knew. Yes, size may have made a difference. One man who stayed a few days with me was a massive offensive guard from UCLA who had heard his grandmother say a few words in Bassa and wanted to imagine her life in Liberia. Oops, I'm starting to tell another story and I do want to get home. And so, full of anticipation, I leave Liberia.

CHAPTER 17

Peace Corps volunteers, whose two or three-year stints were up, departed whenever they felt the urge to go, heading in any direction. A few of the more intrepid made plans to cross the Sahara in a camel caravan via Timbuktu. Not in too much of a hurry. Some chose to stick around to work for Peace Corps, training the in-coming group. Over the years and over the world I have met quite a number of ex-Peace Corps who never quite made it home, settling in far-away places or just living to wander. A few never left. I remember one red-headed, blue-eyed man who convinced himself that he was really a Black man inside. I don't know if the authorities in this Black republic bought that line. Another volunteer, a brilliant music historian and organist who lived far up-country in a walk-in post, returned to Cincinnati, couldn't find a way to adjust, and when I last heard, was desperate to get back to Liberia.

My own first stop was the Canary Islands. As part of Spain, that seemed like a good place to catch some rays and reacclimate myself to European and western ways. It was beautiful, but after a few days, I wondered what I was doing there. And in addition, after boiling and drinking water from a shallow well for two years in Liberia, it was apparently the water of Las Palmas that undid me. By the time I got to my next stop, Casablanca, I was very sick. I may have walked the streets a couple times, but what I mostly remember about Casablanca was the bidet and the patterns on the ceiling of my hotel room while I lay flat out. Paris, or maybe my friend from college, Mary Drain, provided the antidote. She had moved to Paris after college and never left. In fact, years later, when our family lived in Paris for a time, Mary's three French children and our three children played together in parks near her home. There is in Paris a famous brasserie, au Pied de Cochon, noted for its original French onion soup. Mary took me there, not for medicinal purposes, but it sure did the trick. Paris with Mary as my guide was a lot more fun after that.

Next I flew to London which I found to be way too big and bustling with the kind of energy I couldn't muster. I went to the train station in London and made the unusual request to buy a ticket to a small town, you name it, Mr. Ticket Seller, close to the North Sea. He suggested Scarborough and that sounded perfect, Paul Simon's tune already running in my head. Once there, I booked a hotel room right across the street from the roaring sea. Because I may have been the only guest and it was between Christmas and New Years, the host family took me in and treated me royally. Scarborough was just what I needed. In my exuberance to see the countryside I walked miles each day and returned exhausted to great English meals (yes, they can be) at the hotel. I still can't remember what guitar I may have been dragging along with me, but I know I played songs for tips at the hotel's New Year's Eve party and had a great time.

CHAPTER 18

And finally? Finally, I flew to Boston where I would meet up with Carol who was just returning from home after being maid-of-honor at her sister's wedding in Willoughby. Our reunion proved to be a little awkward for a couple of reasons. First, Carol was sharing a flat with two other women and quarters were crowded. And then my friend Denny McDonnell showed up in Boston to greet me after the two years. Remember Cathy Lawless from Lake George who later showed up at Don Bosco on the hill? Denny, as it turned out, had become quite enamored of her, and began seeing her at her girls prep school in New York, long after I was overseas. Cathy and Denny had eloped, and, when they came to Boston, they brought Aelish, their new-born girl. As good as were everyone's intentions, I was more than a bit spooked by all of it. We'll leave it at that and fly home to Willoughby.

My mother by this time had moved out of our family home on Park Avenue and into a two-bedroom apartment. She worked at the Savings and Loan in town and seemed to be doing well. I stayed there with her for only a short time. Another old friend, Tom McCauley, invited me to share an apartment on Murray Hill in Cleveland, a traditionally Italian neighborhood which was lately giving way to off-campus housing for Case Western Reserve. A great place to live. Tom was teaching English at Saint Ignatius High School. I didn't have the first clue what I wanted to do and didn't even want to think about it.

Culture shock is what they call it, and I had it bad. I had no idea how to act among all these white people and felt very out of place and self-conscious in group situations. Tom, bless him, is/was very social, and our place on Murry Hill was a beehive. Difficult to hide out in. I signed up again for substitute teaching in Cleveland to make some money, but this was nothing like the African school I was teaching in just a few months prior. When students let me know they were "Black and Proud," I thought about what a Liberian meant by "black." That meant really black, as in skin coloration. Here was a new context which had much deeper cultural implications.

I had not been back in the states more than a few weeks when the Selective Service notified me that I had been selected, reclassified One-A, and I would be required to report for a physical exam at a specified time…soon. That threw a huge wrench into my already difficult adjustment. My long fight against the Vietnam war and our overall actions in southeast Asia was up to this point largely an internal battle, with the exception of singing protest songs, i.e. preaching to the choir, at a few open-mic coffee houses. Now what? I knew I was not going to Vietnam. Canada or anywhere else in the world was my ace in the hole, but that would be a last resort. I applied for CO status—Conscientious Objector—and began a very long process of trying to define who I was, simple as that.

Fr. Tom Mahoney, newly ordained, at our Park Avenue house around 1966

In recent years my friend, Father Tom Mahoney, sent back to me a folder that he had been keeping, something I had completely forgotten. In it were all the defining essays, official documents, and a raft of letters from friends all over my world attesting to the sincerity and depth of my objections. These were wonderful, humbling, made me cry. And this re-reading was relatively recent. The draft board at the time was not too keen on accepting personal objections. They were looking for membership—Quakers, Jehovah Witnesses, Amish with their long histories of pacifism. Martin Luther King or Ghandhi might not have made the cut. What chance did I have?

The physical exam was scheduled and I stayed up all the night before, drinking and otherwise aspiring to be in the worst physical shape possible without losing consciousness. Consciousness, a very low threshold, as it turned out, was just what the army was looking for. And it appeared as though I was acing their exam. After the written part and many hours of my stripping and their probing, toward the end of the long exam, they asked the group if there were any physical conditions that we were aware of that the examiners would not have found. If so, please step out to be interviewed. I jumped out, sure to think of something, much like waiting for Homadu Jallah to reach the front door.

Off in a small partitioned cubby, a sergeant asked what my ailment was. I had eczema on my fingers, a condition of pealing skin not unlike what my father had when I was growing up. (He regularly rinsed it in gasoline, not the recommended treatment.) With my palms outstretched, I told the examiner that I had been in Africa recently and believed that I had "jungle rot." Those words seemed alarming enough that they went into the report, and I was referred to a dermatologist for a follow-up on another day. I remembered his name, Dr. Leonard Katz, and when I saw him listed in the obituaries just a year ago from this writing, I was compelled to pen a note to his family. At the risk of repetition, this is what I wrote:

"More than fifty years ago, after returning from two years in the Peace Corps, I was classified 1-A and told to report for an Army physical. At the end of a long day, I looked at the eczema on my hands and told the examiner it was "some kind of jungle rot" I had picked up in Africa. They sent me to Dr. Katz.

Dr. Katz asked me what my ailment was, and with no clue as to his position on the war in Vietnam, I said, simply, 'the draft and this horrible war.' He looked at my hands and asked more questions, took notes, but offered no opinion.

Two weeks later my draft board informed me that I was re-classified 4-F, permanently disqualified from the army due to a health condition. That was the only time I met Dr. Katz, but I never forgot his name. With sadness and immense gratitude I read of his passing this morning." 2/10/23

In my short appearance before the draft board, I was asked if I wished to withdraw my application for Conscientious Objector status. I said, "No, please keep it on file, just in case." Could I really have danced my way out of that room full of all those sober faces?

Going Together

CHAPTER 19

*M*aybe my bags were already packed for a new life in Canada. But since they were packed anyway, the day after my draft hearing, the first of April, once more I put my thumb out, this time heading west to San Diego where my brother Bob was stationed in the Navy. Yes, he had left the seminary, too.

There aren't a lot of details to share about that trip and my stay on the west coast. But I think of it as liberating. A huge burden, which had consumed so much of my time and energy in the prior months, was now lifted. I could breathe, and southern California had all the air I was craving. For the next month I explored on bike and foot the ocean, the hills, the city of San Diego and, of course, the zoo. I caddied for one of Bob's Navy roommates who was hoping to qualify for the US Open. We all watched the sunset every night on a rise overlooking the water. At some point we loaded up Bob's old Packard (could have been the last one on the road) and headed to Tiajuana and on to Baja Mexico to camp on the gulf beach. What sticks in my mind most about Baja was staring into a most brilliant panoply of stars stretching across the desert sky. I was conscious of my tiny presence in a vast universe, and that felt very good.

Bob had orders to ship out to a Navy installation in Scotland with a short leave in between. So once again we packed the old car, fondly called the Great White Whale, and headed east toward home in late May. We camped out along the way, sleeping uncomfortably on the wide front and back seats. We picked up a number of colorful hitchhikers, replaced an alternator and radiator at different times, had several conversations with the highway patrol, and limped into Willoughby. The Great White Whale's last hurrah.

Reality and my need to get it in gear were pressing gently but firmly on my psyche. In the middle of my war against the war, I had applied to graduate school in Cincinnati. Growing up my career models had been priests, teachers, and salesmen. I loved math, the physical sciences, and putting things together, but the engineer-fathers I knew were very reserved, wore thick glasses, and their kids didn't play sports. As an undergrad I read literature, and in the Peace Corps, I read hundreds of books. Sociology interested me at one time, and I applied to grad school in that field even while I was still in Africa. If American University had offered me more money, I might have become a sociologist, whatever that is. But now Cincinnati, which I imagined to be warmer and with a friendlier feel than Cleveland, seemed like a good destination. And the English department at the university said I could join them.

Between my return from the west coast and the fall semester at UC, I had to make at least enough money to pay for rent, food, books and a semester's worth of tuition. I couldn't think past the one semester. That summer, while still living on Murray Hill with Tom McCauley, I again painted houses, this time with a slightly more professional crew. The boss also ran a landscaping business, and at first he put me to work behind any number of power mowers. One day of that was enough for me. What I liked about painting was the quiet, especially the kind of quiet you can find two or three stories up on a scaffold, scraping and puttying a window, getting it ready for a final coat. But reading books appealed to me more.

Not far from the campus at UC, I found a house to share with an undergrad senior on the upper floor of a duplex. Carol was in grad school at Boston University at the time, and I think she was also working for Pan Am at Logan Airport. Our visits over the months had been sporadic to say the least. I had a little Opel (a pint-sized German car) that I wouldn't have trusted on I-90 to Boston, so the few trips I made there usually employed my thumb, though I will admit, I was losing my enthusiasm for that mode of transportation.

One of my great strokes of luck came in my first semester at UC. I had signed up for Irish Literature with a formidable Joycean scholar, Hugh Staples, who also happened to be the department head. He allowed me to create an audio program of historical Irish ballads instead of writing a term paper, and I would say he was quite entertained by my presentation. Now, toward the end of the term, he asked me what I had signed up for in the second semester. But I had to tell him that, in spite of my working nights as a bartender, there wouldn't be enough coin in the coffers for me to stay on. "Well," he said, "we'll see about that." Maybe late that day or the next, I met the director of the teaching assistant program who offered a stipend to cover housing, board and books, along with the gift of two freshman composition classes per semester. No more bartending and I could put my budding career as a house-painter on hold.

But it was hard work. My graduate course-load was two or three classes per semester which required me to read, on average, a book a day. In addition, the freshman composition courses that I taught asked for, of course, compositions, which I had to read carefully. As I looked around at my graduate colleagues and toward my bright young professors, struggling to publish or perish, I realized into what a cauldron of intellectual academia and personal angst I had dropped in.

Those who worked hard also played hard. It was my good friend John Druska whom I met in Hugh Staples's class, who introduced me to the flip side of grad school. A strip of bars and small retail stores lined a street adjacent to the Cincinnati campus. One of these places featured the best blue-grass music around, and the house was packed every night, packed with the brain power of the university. They let themselves out at night to knock out a few brain cells with drink and swap spouses on their way out the door. It could get wild. John Druska was the poet-in-residence at the university and a doctoral student on a more equal plane with the tenured elite. He liked his drink, but there was nothing anxious about him. He enjoyed experiencing the wild, but it was more to gather fodder for his imaginative writing. John and I would play chess in the park when the weather was warm. I sang at his wedding.

I honestly have no idea what kind of a teacher I was or what effect I may have had on these first-year college students. University of Cincinnati at the time had "open admissions," meaning that anyone who completed high school could enroll, and also meaning that this wasn't Harvard. But I had many bright and talented students from very diverse backgrounds. I worked hard to help them legitimize their opinions and the ways in which they had already found to express their maturing voices. Sometimes I thought I was too hard on them; other times too easy. On my very first day I unwittingly took a seat in the front of the class while I waited for the students to come in. After we were assembled, I stood up, turned around, and introduced myself as their instructor. That brought some good-natured hoots from the disbelievers. "Oh, yeah, sure." Then I handed out the syllabus.

A couple of mechanically-gifted students came over to my place on occasion to help me keep the Opel on the road. A girl from my class, Joyce, accompanied me on classical guitar for a graduate project of mine involving Dryden's operas. She also wrote in naturally crystal-clear sentences that should be the envy of any graduate literature student. I remember one class of mostly in-training nurses. They knew each other well and had fun. They were also excellent students.

Three of the nurses must have taken pity on my solitary ways and asked if I'd like to join them on a Sunday evening, to go bowling or to a roller rink. I can't remember which because we never got there. The girls picked me up on their way from hospital rounds. It was a chilly night with rain turning to sleet and ice. The girls told me that they would need to make a brief stop home before heading to the rink, or was it the alley? As we were coming down one of the many Cincinnati hills, the car went into a slide, which I'm sure the young driver had never experienced before. She slammed on the brakes. Hard. Without letting up. The car, with its wheels locked, floated as if in slow motion, down the hill toward a row of parked cars. And bam! We got the first one. No serious damage and no one hurt. We found ourselves in front of a small Baptist church which was crowded for Sunday night services. The girls seemed reluctant to get out in search of the owner of the vehicle we plowed into, and with good reason. The girls were Black and this church was all white. And if that wasn't cause for timidity, they then told me that the reason they had to stop at home was that, after stripping off their nurses' uniforms, they didn't have much on under their long coats and had intended to change. It was up to me to go in and stop the service, me, a white guy with three naked Black girls in long coats. Yes, I did it, but, fortunately, there's no more to the story. Sorry. It all worked out, although I know you can imagine many other possible scenarios and endings.

A few visitors came to see me in Cincinnati. I can remember taking my mother out to dinner at Ted Kluszewski's steakhouse. I recall that because I was required to be fitted for a coat to enter (It was a little large for me.), but how my mother got to Cincy or where she stayed? No clue. Tom McCauley, my roommate from Murray Hill, came down in his brand new Corolla. That I remember because my dog Brian Boru puked all over the console and gear shift in the new car. Tom asked me anyway to be his best man which I took seriously and couldn't imagine being the best man standing next to him. Of course I said yes. He was marrying Lonnie who was Denny McDonnell's girlfriend when I lived with Denny "on the hill" before Cathy Lawless paid her visit. It does get complicated.

Carol took the bus to Cincinnati once or twice. In the summer between my two years in grad school, Carol flew around the world with her brother, compliments of Pan Am. And in the fall she escorted her neighbors, the Pallisters, on their trip to the British Isles and stayed on for awhile in Scotland after the Pallisters returned. That's a long way from southern Ohio.

My work over the summer between years did involve some brief house-painting in Cincinnati, but the dreaded written and oral exams, which I would take in the spring, ever loomed, and I had to read as much as I could. That exam to earn a Masters in Literature was in lieu of a thesis, which I don't believe was an option at the time. Probably April of my second year I sat for the five-hour written exam consisting of thirty essay questions on the subject of a thousand years of literature. I'm sure no one could answer all thirty. Well, I'm not so sure. A German woman and an east Indian had what seemed to me to be an encyclopedic hold on the whole millennium. They probably were not required to appear for the follow-up two-hour oral exam. I was. Elliott Gould's movie "Getting Straight" had been out for two years, and I felt I was living that scene of his oral exam, crazy as it was. Six professors from every corner of the millennium threw questions like darts related to their expertise. But once the Beowulf guy and the Elizabethan had made their best shot, they sat back while Tom Jones and early novelists came to the fore. You can see how it went all the way to the twentieth century. Two hours. I think I was lucky in my grad school timing. The year before, the UC English department passed only a handful out of the twenty-five who sat the exams, and there was a minor uproar. I knew they couldn't do that, not two years in a row. I had a couple professor friends in the room, too, and I think they convinced the others that, not only should I pass, but also be recommended to pursue a PhD. I thanked them, but they had gone too far. I needed light. And maybe a job.

Ah, another breath of fresh April air. The exam was behind me and I was beginning to enjoy a little unencumbered free time. One day one of the students from downstairs of the duplex knocked on my door to ask to use the telephone. He said he wanted to call the phone company to have a phone installed. Odd timing, I thought, since there were only a few weeks until the end of the term and his graduation. Eric said he needed the phone because his undergraduate thesis in design or engineering required him to find someone to follow fifty pages of his directions. In this case directions on how to make a banjo from scratch. He wanted to put an ad in the newspaper with a phone number. "Eric," I said, "you don't need a phone, you need me." And that was the beginning of a lifetime of making musical instruments. Three weeks later I appeared before his own congregation of professors and let the banjo, such as it was, attest to the clarity of Eric's instructions.

One other niggling obstruction stood in the way of my exit from Cincinnati. About a month before the end of the semester, while I was still teaching my own classes, I got a call from someone who had bought the duplex from my landlord. She told me that I would have to be out of the apartment in two weeks. "That would be impossible," I said. "I have another month of school." "Too bad," says she, "You gotta get out." I told her exactly which day in one month that I would be leaving, held off sending my last month's rent and otherwise ignored her request. On the fateful day, two weeks past <u>her</u> deadline, I was nearly done packing when she and two tough-looking guys showed up to block my way upstairs and collect the rent. With a polite "excuse me" I sidled past one of them on the stairs and grabbed a box or two. By the time I came back down, three police squad cars were in the front yard. An officer asked what was going on. She, the new owner, yelled that I was trespassing and that I owed her rent money. I told the officer I owed this woman nothing, taking into account the cost of my emotional distress. In his most professional voice, the officer informed the woman that this was a civil case and that she would have to take it up in court. As for me, I didn't go back to get the last of my shirts upstairs. I jumped in the car, narrowly escaping another mama lion, and headed north.

CHAPTER 20

*B*ack in Willoughby, aged twenty-six, Carol and I were now at least living once again in the same town, nine years after we had first met. Soon we hatched a plan to travel to Scotland together in August and live there for a time. My brother Bob had lived in Campbelltown with the US Navy on the Argyle peninsula and was eager to join me in playing music in pubs. Carol had lived for a time in Edinburgh and knew the more practical ropes. She had a friend who owned a large flat in the Morningside area of Edinburgh where we could take two rooms and share the common space. In the meantime, over the summer, we'd have to work and save every penny.

It would be safe to say I painted houses that summer, but I think I've already told about all the jobs I remember. What I do know is that I worked for hourly wages and got paid every two weeks. Carol, on the other hand, worked as a waitress at two high-end restaurants. People in those days paid cash and tipped in cash, so every night she'd empty her purse and pockets onto her bed and count out $150-$200, which, added to her hourly wages, amounted to about five times more than my job could account for. She was cashing in, you might say, on her patrons' penchant for alcohol and her youthful good looks. But neither of us were at all tempted to stick around.

Sometime in August, in time for the Edinburgh Festival, Carol and I left Willoughby (together!), and were soon joined by brother Bob who was coming in from northern Virginia. Bob got the closet of a room and seemed pleased. Carol and I had a front room with a large bay window overlooking Morningside Road. The other three rooms in the house were inhabited by a Scottish singer/pianist and his girlfriend; a brilliant journalist from northern England who could get your life story in minutes and never reveal a thing about herself; and finally a reserved and friendly Canadian girl. What a wonderful collection of folks that turned out to be. My mother referred to our arrangement as "shacking up", but I was already "fallen away" and, in hindsight, this looked like the beginning of the new norm for developing relationships.

The owner of the flat was a young married woman who was well-educated and well-connected. I'd say she was upward bound, except that I think she was born in that realm. Marilyn had something administrative to do with the Edinburgh Festival, the annual gathering of Europe's best in music, arts, and drama. She could get us tickets for events or provide unique angles on some of the venues. One day, she told us that there would be a rehearsal of Mahler's 4th, with Leonard Bernstein and the London Philharmonic at the performing hall. We could slip in with the large chorus and take a seat. That I did, a nice seat in the balcony, but Carol and I had become separated, and when I looked down at the stage, there she was among the altos, paying close attention to Bernstein's baton. She maintained the charade for the duration of the rehearsal, but when Bernstein asked the altos to stay behind at the end, Carol wisely disappeared from stage.

When Bob came, he and I went to work practicing and putting together lists of songs. My banjo was a challenging new addition to the act. Bob had done some busking, as in playing on street corners, but Edinburgh's weather and its more (more than Glasgow or Dublin, say) proper and crusty ways didn't lend well to putting out the hat. We tried dragging our instruments into a few pubs, but we really needed some kind of introduction. We made contact with a minor music agent who did bookings, and we went to his place in a neighborhood not far from the Firth of Forth (sorry, had to put it in, "not far from the Firth of Forth"). Downstairs he had a music studio. He asked us something that sounded like "Air ye a Jewo?" I harkened back to our Catholic backgrounds, but was confused by the question. Bob, who had a natural gift for picking up language, told me he was asking if we were a duo. Yes. We played a few songs in his basement studio, and he must have liked what he heard. He brought out a bottle of Scotch whiskey with a type-written label and poured out three generous tumblers full. Thus was the beginning of our music careers in Edinburgh.

THE FIRST TRI: AS A YOUNG MAN

The beauty of playing music in Edinburgh for me was the very strict hours established for public houses, i.e. pubs. They were open from noon to two, closed again until 7:30 p.m. Open again until the last call when the bell rang promptly at ten. An astonishing amount of alcohol can go down in two-plus hours—the sidewalks on the way home were terrible, worse for different reasons than Paris sidewalks of the same time. Leave it at that. So our gigs were, max, two hours long, and that left a lot of free-time during the day to explore a town we came to enjoy so much. We weren't rolling in dough, but we could eat and pay the rent, and who can ask for more? Well....

We walked many of the beautiful Edinburgh parks, and one day I discovered among tree trimmings two branch logs that had what were to me interesting colors at the core. I suppose the inclination to make things hadn't left me since my banjo-building days just a few months prior. One piece was holly; the other a darker wood, more like olive but not likely that. I imagined a chess set, and with a little vise, a knife or two, a saw and rasp files, I went to work at a small table within our flat. The set had a nautical theme, one king a sea-serpent, the other a whale. The queens were sharks. It's a little bit of my history that I treasure. This memory carries with it a slight tinge of guilt, however, because I can still hear Mrs. McCloud's broom rapping on the floor from below. What could we possibly be doing up there with all that pounding and scraping?

Edinburgh was surprisingly small as we got to know it. We met people every night that we played, and we made good friends within the musical community—fiddlers, banjo players, pipers, pianists, singers. We hauled a piano up three flights to our flat on Morningside and played in when we weren't playing out. We had two or three standing gigs on the Royal Mile and bought a low-tech PA system, small enough to carry with our instruments when we squeezed onto public buses. A sight we must have been. The Waverly and Yellow Carvel are two pubs that stand out in my memory, maybe because we played there often. But we also were booked by our agent to play some rather odd events.

One night we were scheduled to play a place called the "Purple Palace," without a clue as to what sort of pub that might be. It turned out to be more the anti-pub. A group of well-mean-

The Lost Nation Revival's last stand at the Waverly on the Royal Mile

ing church ladies had decided to serve a full holiday meal for all the down-and-outers they could collect off the streets. Bob and I would be the entertainment. Problem was, none of these folks coming in for dinner, mostly men, had eaten solid foods in a long time. And out came the dishes of roast beef, turnips, mashed potatoes, and rich homemade desserts. As we played on, we got a view from the stage of how a good idea can really go bad. By the end, the men were staggering back out onto the streets, apparently in much worse condition than when they had come in.

On a more pleasant note, Bob and I traveled several times to a mining town called Gore Bridge to play at the Gore Bridge Burns Club, a collection of hard-core socialists who loved our music. Our friend Austin got us there, quite a ways from Edinburgh, in his van, and the three of us always had a jolly time. As you know, people will often begin a joke with the phrase, "Have you heard the one about…?" And, if the answer is yes, they sit back down. We don't do that with songs, do we? You would like to hear a song again, <u>especially</u> if you've heard it before. At the Burns Club one man was sure to tell the same joke each time we were there and probably every night in between. In fact, the crowd begged for it. And it was funnier at every telling. On our last outing there, along with the haggis, neeps, tatties and good whiskey, Bob and I received a lifetime membership to the Gore Bridge Burns Club.

Carol usually accompanied us on our in-town gigs and did a sound-check in front of the microphones with her rendition of "I Love you Because," getting about that far before dissolving into a giggle. In October her cousin came for a visit and the two of them went off to the west coast and the islands beyond, a trip that proved quite fortuitous. When hitchhiking in the rain on the Isle of Mull, they were picked up by a woman going home to her place in Bunessan, not far from Iona at the far western end of the island. She was assertive, I'm told, saying "You can't be out in weather like this, you'll have to stay the night with me." On the way she half turned around and asked Carol if she would be willing to house-sit from January to March while she was visiting family in New Zealand. They were now old friends of a half hour. In addition, Euphemia told Carol that friends of hers in Edinburgh, the Lord and Lady Baxter, needed a chef to get them through the holidays, and she would get Carol that job as long as she promised to come back in January. The rest of the story is mostly Carol's, but the Baxters owned a car dealership, and soon we had wheels at our disposal.

THE FIRST TRI: AS A YOUNG MAN

On New Year's Eve, my 27th birthday, Bob and I played a memorable gig at the Yellow Carvel. Every musician we knew and a number we didn't joined us on stage that night of raucous musical debauchery. Don't remember much about the long walk home.

But Bob and I in the new year were getting played out. We weren't working on anything new, Carol was going off to the Isle of Mull, and Bob was starting to think about moving on, moving back. It had been a blast and we gave it one last stand at the Waverly. Our friend Austin let the word out that this was it, our swan song, and everyone came. The place was packed.

Bob's six month visa ran out and he returned to the states. I applied for a six-month extension with the excuse that I was doing research in Scottish ethnomusicology, not too far off the truth. It worked, and in Carol's absence, I took a job in a French restaurant, got paid under the table and was introduced to a colorful group of middle easterners who were my fellow waiters and bartenders. I learned a lot from them about serving properly and really enjoyed their parties in the off-hours. The owner of the restaurant lived on the third floor, a lonely alcoholic whom I met only once, the day he hired me. That day, downstairs, Zach, the maître d', suggested I shave off the scruff. I have no pride and cleaned up well enough for the new job.

Garcon de l'Ecosse

In early March, before Euphemia's return. I joined Carol on Mull. We fed Euphemia's forty chickens, collected and distributed eggs to neighbors, and took the five dogs on long hikes every day across the hills and along the coast. Our archivist/journalist roommate from Edinburgh, Leslie, arrived for a few days and swam with the seals. We came to know and enjoy Lady Freeman from up the road. She was eighty and didn't miss a beat when she joined us on our treks. Most days we were also joined by a young local girl named Sue and her two collies. Sue, who was anything but local in her outlook, was committed to living close to the earth. She spun her own yarn, a mixture of sheep's wool and dog fur, and wove beautifully designed material. In a side note, Sue's two dogs later made an appearance in the movie "Local Hero," a delightful 1983 comedy dealing with the interface of big oil America and small-town Scotland starring Burt Lancaster. This picture is worth a thousand words. Altogether our time on Mull stands out as a magical month.

In spite of my many proposals up till then, I think it was during our stay on Mull that all Carol's "maybes," became "OK, let's plan it." And so we did. I wrote a letter to Carol's father, asking for his approval in my seeking her hand in marriage. Formal? Yes, I know. Effective? Immensely. He cried, I'm told, perhaps relieved that his twenty-seven-year-old daughter had run out of countries to traverse and was slowing down long enough for the likes of me to catch up to her. We would be coming home in July and get married in August.

But first we had some miles to cover. Back in Edinburgh, we had a jeweler craft two wedding rings, making it a little easier to circumnavigate the matronly women we would encounter at the youth hostels of Ireland. Next we found a local man who reconditioned bicycles and purchased two five-speeds. The plan, if you could call it that, was to load up everything we owned, including a strapped-on guitar, and tour Ireland via Wales, then down the east coast of England, a ferry over to Rotterdam, on to Paris, then down to Provence and up the Rhone valley to Luxembourg from where we would fly to Iceland, bike the moonscape there and finally land in Cleveland. That run-on sentence alone exhausts me. What were we thinking? Hey, we were young. So now I should tell you about the alliterative strain of the rain round the ring of Kerry; or the night a horse tromped on our sleeping selves, camped in a defunct youth hostel near Marseilles; or the look of two weather-beaten Spartans cruising the Riviera on loaded-down bikes among soft pink sun-bathers. But look, I have a wedding to attend to and a little more than a month to plan it. Got to get home.

Bonjeur de la Riviera

Settling In

CHAPTER 21

*"Such a weddin' ya never did see,
Had three green beans and a black-eyed pea."*

We were home the first of July and a few days later our Scottish friend Austin hitched in from Manitoba where he had recently been working. Austin and I spent the next weeks laying a patio at Carol's parents' house and otherwise getting the back yard in shape to host the grand reception. Carol worked on wedding arrangements—the dress, the cake, the food, the flowers, the guest lists, the church, the minister, the organist. Every evening after Carol's father returned from work, we would all have a wine-tasting so we could get the formula just right. That along with his homemade hummus and pita from the Lebanese bakery.

Weddings and funerals, these are the events that bring all manner of folk together. As I look back at all that I've written, I realize that on our wedding day in August we gathered friends from Scotland, John Carroll, Cincinnati, Don Bosco, Africa, Borromeo Seminary, and the swimming pool. And that's before adding in our families and family friends and dozens of cousins. The story of my life stretched across the back garden. Brother Bob was my best man. We sang a duet at the church ceremony and later did our best act at the reception. Carol's sister Pat, an artist who had designed the invitation and arranged the flowers, was her matron-of-honor. The party went on for days it seemed, culminating in my new mother-in-law driving a bunch of us to Chicago and Union Pier Michigan for what I kiddingly call our "honeymoon."

A local clothier and good friend, Oliver Smith, had fitted Bob and me for our very trendy, mid-seventies wedding outfits—plaid pants and linen coats. You'd have to see the pictures. Oliver told us at the time that there was an available apartment above his store in downtown Willoughby. Built in 1864, the Wilson Building had four apartments and four offices above and two retail stores below, including Oliver's clothing store and the larger Milmine's appliance store. We took it and I agreed to be the custodian of the building. Our rent was set at $25/month. Carol, who had done a masters in teaching at Boston University and student taught in Boston, began her teaching in the middle school of the Willoughby district the next month.

I went to work for a company that installed in-ground sprinklers, and when it got cold, I went inside to a factory that made copies of Shaker furniture, good stuff out of cherry, for the tourist market in New England. Neither job probably fit whatever nebulous career plans I may have harbored, but you can learn new things wherever you look. I had completed all my education courses except for student-teaching before skipping out on my fourth year at John Carroll. Since then, I had taught two years in Liberia, two years at the University of Cincinnati, and put in some time subbing in Cleveland. Ah, says the education department at JCU, fine, but we haven't seen you teach under our auspices. And so in the spring, if I wanted to be certified, I would be required to student teach. What that meant to me was that I would be spending $800 to teach someone else's classes at Beachwood High School. Barbara was my "master teacher," and we got along well. She and I had been teaching about the same number of years, and I would later have her own son in my class at another school. I tried not to grumble too much.

Carol wasn't having any more fun than I was in her first year of teaching. Both of us suffered from the effects of the "open classroom" which took down the walls while leaving ill-prepared teachers wandering through herds of noisy adolescents. The latest thing in education was short-lived: the walls soon went back up.

In the late spring, now fully certified, I found out from a neighbor on River Street that a teaching position in English would be open at University School, an all-boys private school on the east side of Cleveland, in Shaker Heights. I didn't know much about US, as it's called, but I didn't hesitate to call on them. Beachwood had offered me a job, part-time, three classes and three preparations, for not much money. An offer I put on the shelf. At University School I met with the headmaster and the Shaker campus director as well as several teachers. This was an impressive place, and as the day went on, I found myself really wanting this job. The campus director, Bob Schwab, wanted to talk about my bicycling, and he was particularly interested in my friendship with Gretta Pallister, a well-known birder and naturalist. I liked everything about this place, and, considering my life story, I did know something about boys. Ironically, they couldn't have cared less about my teaching certification.

CHAPTER 22

A few months before my interview with US, a friend from New York had called to tell Carol and me about an interesting job that she saw posted at the Columbia student center. JCPenney and Celanese Corporations were looking for a couple, presumably a married couple, to escort twelve college students on a cross-country bicycle trip, New York to San Francisco. Sounded interesting and we applied. The PR people who were planning the trip were surprised to hear from a mid-western couple, far from where they posted the ad. They flew us to JFK airport for an interview with a corporate headhunter who must have liked our folksy midwestern ways and recognized that we knew bicycling and, as teachers, had the summer off. I think he hired us before we flew back home from the airport two hours later.

We were to begin our cross-country journey in early June, but I hadn't heard back from University School about the middle school teaching position. The day before we left for New York I called Bob Schwab, director of the K-8 campus, and asked him if US had come to a decision. I did point out, without sounding threatening I hope, that there were a number of schools between New York and San Francisco and I was looking for a job. He said he'd get back to me. Two hours later he called and asked me to come over to the school to sign a teaching contract. Thirty years later I would retire from teaching at US. I had no inkling of that then, but the news that day was a big relief.

Dipping the rear tires in the Atlantic

In New York we began to see what the trip would entail. The routes were all laid out, but by Penney and Celanese junior executives, not bicyclists. The idea was to beat "Bike-centennial" to the punch. That was a much-advertised celebration of the 1976 bicentennial coming the next year. They named our effort "The Great American Bike Tour" and measured our success in the number of newspaper articles, TV spots, and audiences we would reach. On the way across the country, we would be stopping at every Penney's store from coast to coast that happened to be within spitting distance of old Route 40. There were a lot of stores in those days, and we would be doing our bicycle safety show at malls and shopping strips. The first week in New York was spent with some writers from Sesame Street who sized up our talent and cast us in a fifteen-minute show. I played guitar, one cyclist played clarinet, another electric piano, while the rest danced about for the little kids with scripted suggestions on how to be safe on a bicycle. As you can imagine, the criteria for choosing the cyclists had more to do with how they looked on Penney's bicycles and in Celanese threads than how they would manage to put in an average of 75 miles per day on the road.

As a send-off we were treated to lunch at the Four Seasons restaurant and tea in the afternoon with Ginger Rogers at her New York apartment, cameras blazing. We followed the tradition of dipping our rear tires in the Atlantic the next day, and off we went. Carol and I were responsible for driving a twenty-eight-foot Winnebago, stripped out and outfitted with shelves to carry the cyclists' luggage and spare parts. The planners imagined that we would be following just behind the group at twelve miles per hour, and we'd all be together all the time. Doesn't work that way. Cyclists travel at very different rates, and moving this monster of a truck at the speed of the cyclists is just plain dangerous. Unaware and angry drivers behind us would fly past the Winnebago and then need to pull in quickly where the slowest members of our group were trundling along. We soon developed our own rhythm. Carol and I would take turns biking or driving. In the morning, we would establish where everyone would meet for lunch, set the group on their way, while one or the other of us would shop for fifty or a hundred dollars-worth of lunch fixings, maybe do some of the group's laundry, then speed ahead till we passed the well-spaced cyclists to get to our designated meeting place and lay out the food for the hungry lot of them. Where we ran into difficulty was doing our safety show at malls that didn't open until 10 a.m. Starting out to cover 75 or 100 miles at eleven or noon made for an exhausting afternoon.

There were some very quirky complications involved in this parade. A crew of film-makers appeared at various locations, hired to make a movie of the event. They got in our way at times with their requests for us to take risks along the road to get just the right shots. And it didn't help that one of the cyclists fell in love with a young gripper. In addition, the Huffy Corporation of Dayton, which manufactured the bikes for Penney's, sent a few mechanics to follow us in a van, a boondoggle for sure, but purportedly to see how their bikes held up. The original group of us and the twelve cyclists had grown to the size of an unruly herd of cats.

You get the picture. I don't need to cover the trail from coast to coast. It did work in the end, and I would have been happy to turn north once we hit California and keep going. The kids became very good cyclists and worked hard to accomplish this unique summer challenge. I would love to hear their own accounting of the bike tour. On the last day we rode from Sacramento where it was 95 degrees to San Francisco which was 55 and fogged in. We dipped our front wheels into the Pacific and ate cake on the chilly beach, cameras whirring. One of our cyclists, of course the prettiest one but a great choice, appeared on the Johnny Carson show to finish off this one very long Penney's commercial. Carol and I retreated to the Sawtooth Mountains of Idaho to hide out for a few days and trout-fish with her aunt and uncle at their cabin. School would start for us in a week or two.

Considering the responsibility we took on, Carol and I insisted on an adult wage, considerably more than what the cyclists were getting for their summer jobs. The whole group, including us, had received a daily stipend plus the bikes and the clothes, etc. Carol and I were paid in a lump sum at the end, not a massive trove, but more than we had ever been able to finger at one time before. Inflation was ridiculous in the mid-seventies and saving it was a fool's errand. "Buy land, they're not making any more of that," said Will Rodgers. Or was it Roy? Fred? Anyway, that fall we started looking.

The towers of University School

CHAPTER 23

When I first started teaching, I thought I would not only be able to recall every one of the students I ever had, but also put them in the context of the class they were in. My first group of seventh and eighth graders in the fall of 1975 would be in their sixties now, close to retirement age. That was nearly fifty years ago, and you can be sure that I would draw a complete blank if one were to tap me on the shoulder tomorrow and say hi. But there are many exceptions, and I can still conjure images of their adolescent selves when I read that one of my students is on the board of trustees now, or another has published a book, or his face appears in today's obituaries. I read, too, about the accomplishments or athletic prowess of their children and grandchildren who, more than likely, also attend or have attended University School.

What really stands out when I think about my first year at University School is the enduring friendships of my teaching colleagues that I have enjoyed over these many years. Some have passed on, of course, many are enjoying retirement and keeping very much alive, but, unbelievably, a few are still at work more than fifty years later, assisting on the field, doing special projects, driving the bus to sporting events. There is continuity to the school which runs deep. Critics might scoff at what they call the "old-boys" network, but when two grads of US meet, even generations apart, they will find much in common because teachers or stories about teachers still abound, the maintenance staff still maintains, sometimes sons joining fathers on the staff, and familiar cooks are still preparing home-style lunches.

US had been around a long time when I got there in '75, a fine old school, but rather set in its ways. The likes of my boss, Bob Schwab, his assistant Stephen Jones, and headmaster Rowland McKinley were terrific leaders who set an admirable pace toward making the school excellent in education and yet sensitive to the needs of individual boys. They were my mentors and good friends. They were alive with learning in their own pursuits and always eager to share their passion for exploration. Many of the teachers in the middle school at that time were about my age, bright and full of energy. University School was always a very good school. With these young teachers and under the effective leadership of the administrators mentioned above, I believe US became a happier place to go to school.

It seems to me that most of those hoping to become teachers don't think too much about landing a job in "middle school." For me, personally, it all depended on who was willing to offer me a job. US made the offer and I found I was made for teaching middle school. It fit. I could engage in all kinds of learning, my own and others', and my language didn't devolve into the esoteric abstractions of academia. I came to believe that this age of early adolescence is a critical pivot point in life. As mentioned earlier, the great cultures of the world have concluded the same with their attention to rites of passage at this age of 12 to 14 years. It's a sensitive time, full of self-consciousness and social angst. Consider my own experiences in the seventh and eighth grades. Rarely does someone look back and announce "Those were the happiest days of my life." Hugely important, but most of us want to do all we can to bury all that self-doubt, deep as we can.

CHAPTER 24

With our "Great American Bike Tour" cash still burning a hole in our proverbial pockets, we added to it in my first year of teaching, and it helped that I had a side gig as janitor of the Wilson building where we lived over Milmine's appliance store in Willoughby. Optimistically we spent a few weekends checking out the real estate listings in neighboring Ashtabula County, close to home but the land much cheaper. We would call a real estate agent late in the week who provided the addresses of parcels of land for sale. We then hiked the properties on our late fall weekends, weighing the positives and negatives of each one as we went. It was like walking in parks that had no paths. We kept coming back to one place, maybe the first piece we had looked at. Half the property was field and woods on one side of the road, the site of a burned-down house, with a large tilting barn in its last throes against gravity. A smaller parcel was on the other side of the road. Here was an open field that had been cultivated in recent years, and from the road you could see a bank of trees and woods beyond. What you could not see is an escarpment just beyond those trees, dropping down to Rock Creek, a tributary of the Grand River which covers two counties and ultimately flows into Lake Erie at Fairport Harbor. Three quarters of a mile of winding river snaked its way through the forty-acre plot. This was bottomland, so inaccessible across the river that large hardwood trees had escaped the ravages of the chain saw and no grazing cattle had taken out the understory.

This was it. Still is. But we were interested only in the piece across the road that so well hid the river behind the small bare field. The whole property was owned by a judge in Cleveland who probably bought it for hunting or as a speculative investment. If we offered, he'd take. Carol and I could only afford half of this parcel, twenty acres, and we didn't want to ask the owner to further divide. So we solicited family and friends and created an informal and very homemade version of a condo association, divvying it all up by percentages of ownership based on the number of acres each went in for. Carol and I, when said and done, became half owners. Five others were part owners of the other half.

It wasn't as though we were trying to create a private version of the metroparks which surround Cleveland, nor was it to make a killing on a real estate flip. There was at the time a very real fear that the world was running out of oil. OPEC cut the supply of oil production and people everywhere were turning down the thermostat. "Mother Earth News" was telling us to return to the land, hunker down and work your way to self-sufficiency and sustainability. The "forty acres and a mule" was for us more like forty acres, a rich woods and a long stretch of river. We would be ready for the worst, but the

THE FIRST TRI: AS A YOUNG MAN

Planting seeds…

dire predictions of our return to hunting and gathering didn't pan out. Life in Willoughby and at our respective schools went on.

In the late spring of 1977, after a rather brutal winter, Carol and I planted three or four thousand tiny pine trees along Dodge Road, the front of our property. I think it was closer to five thousand, but that seems over the top and nearly impossible to get done in one or two weekends. The father of a teaching colleague at

US was the forester for northeastern Ohio. I don't actually know what that means, but he was giving out trees that the state provided, and we got a bunch. Individually, each plant was about twelve inches tall, six in greenery, six in roots. Carol was eight months pregnant at the time, carrying the first of our ten-pound babies. I don't know how she managed to bend over, but we got into a rhythm that had me using a spade to divide the earth and Carol following with bundles of tiny trees, setting one into each crevice and stomping it closed. Walk two paces and repeat. We got three rows done across the thousand-foot front, three more rows along the three-hundred-foot north side, plus a number in the field near where we imagined a barn or a driveway. I never did the math, but that is a lot of trees. Luckily for us, it rained nearly steadily for the next two weeks. Those trees today make a fence that is more than seventy feet tall.

CHAPTER 25

*J*ust a few weeks after the plantings and that welcome deluge, our first son, Colin, was born, 7-7-77. And that brings me to a point of departure. My life till now, thirty years old and the father of our first child, is full of the stories my children could never know unless I've told them. I've tried to tell a few. Now it will be up to them to plumb their own much fresher memories, maybe make it a biography, if they're interested, instead of an autobiography. They've been on the journey with us for a long time, so many of my later stories are also their stories.

When I mentioned this project recently to a friend, she recommended a book called *Essential Questions*. The author presented an anthropologist's method on how to conduct and interview your parents and grandparents, so that you discover the essential stories. Chapter by chapter, questions were listed and blank pages were included for the interviewer to record what was discovered. The goal was to get those memories out, but there wasn't much attention paid to what you do with them once they've surfaced. Do you put them in a bank of audio or video recordings? A notebook full of quotes? A long narrative? Ah, there's the rub. So *Essential Questions* wasn't for me, the opposite really. The stories weren't pried out of my aging self, and I chose a narrative style for my own telling. I hope in reading this my family isn't disappointed in my not responding to their thoughtful prompts. If something is missing, I'd like to think they will have plenty of time to sit me down, ask the essential questions and add to what's already here.

In hindsight it's been easy to write a formula for what constitutes a good life. Easier if you don't account for tragedy which lurks every minute around every corner. We have been so lucky. A preacher corrected me once when I said that. "No," he said, "you've been blessed." Okay, I'll take it. But here's the outline, carefully designed while looking backward. It's the thirty-thirty-thirty plan. In your first years you grow up, acquire all the education possible, formal or hard-knocks. Travel whatever part of the world you can reach. Fall in love and make that commitment. If you've come that far, then have a baby and begin to experience parenthood. Part II is a lot of work. Joyful work, we hope. The work of being a mother or father, and doing all you can to give them the best education affordable, so their worlds are widened beyond what you can even imagine. The work of making a living while pursuing your own education and interests. And the work of self-restraint, trying to distinguish what is important from what is simply pleasurable. That means saving, as in money, all you are able to save, because in Part III, after the first thirty and then thirty more, you are now sixty, and, even though you know what's coming, you can re-live the best of it and go beyond, immerse yourself in projects long shelved, travel, and teach and cherish your grandchildren. Enjoy being the elder. There's dignity in it.

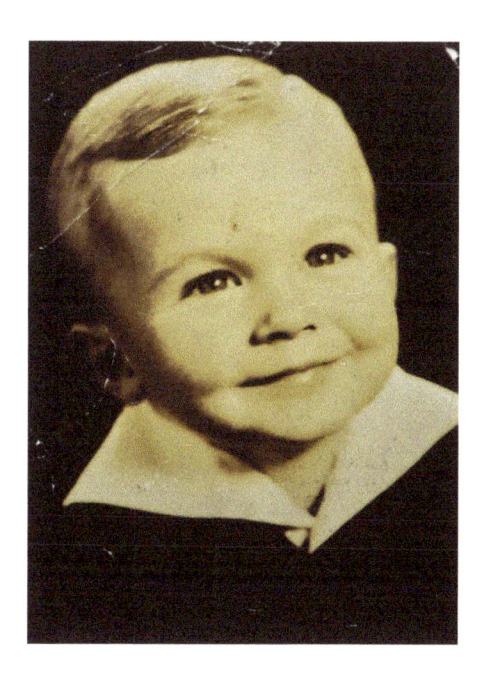

Well, that's it, or I thought it was, until now that I'm done writing and realize none of this would have been written if my children and families had not banded together, which, I now concede, was for my own good. So my deep thanks to Colin and Carrie, Thomas and Andrea, and Ellana and Helen. My applause, but please know I'm also handing off the baton to each of you.

Good luck on the next lap and much love always, D.

A special thanks to my friend, Marilyn Doerr, PhD. She is a wonderful teacher of us all, a colleague in our halcyon days at school, and lately, a very careful and kindly reader. Always kindly, yes, but ever insisting on the best each of us can do.

And the rest of the story? What follows is fifty years of marriage this month to that girl named Carol, whom I met standing next to the pop-stand a long time ago. Yes, I am blessed…and damn lucky.

Milton Keynes UK
Ingram Content Group UK Ltd.
UKHW022140201124
451425UK00021B/372